STEAKS, CHOPS, ROASTS & RIBS

STEAKS, CHOPS, ROASTS & RIBS

Packed with delicious recipes for the oven and barbecue

p

This is a Parragon Publishing Book
First published in 2005

Parragon Publishing
Queen Street House
4 Queen Street
Bath BA1 1HE
United Kingdom

This edition designed by Talking Design Ltd, Worthing, West Sussex, UK.

ISBN: 1-40546-039-3

Printed in Indonesia

NOTE
This book uses imperial, metric, or US cup measurements. Follow the same units of measurement
throughout; do not mix metric and imperial. All spoon measurements are level: teaspoons are
assumed to be 5 ml and tablespoons are assumed to be 15 ml. Unless otherwise stated, milk is
assumed to be whole, eggs and individual vegetables such as potatoes are medium, and pepper is
freshly ground black pepper.

The times given for each recipe are an approximate guide only because the preparation times may
differ accordingly to the techniques used by different people and the cooking times may vary as a
result of the type of oven and other equipment used.

Recipes using raw or very lightly cooked eggs should be avoided by infants, the elderly, pregnant
women, convalescents and anyone suffering from an illness. Pregnant and breast-feeding women
are advised to avoid eating peanuts and peanut products.

CONTENTS

INTRODUCTION	6
1 STEAKS	12
2 CHOPS	66
3 ROASTS	120
4 RIBS	174
5 SIDES	216
INDEX	254

INTRODUCTION

Even in prehistoric times, meat formed part of the human diet, especially once people had mastered the art of making fire and could therefore cook it to make it more tender and palatable. Almost every cuisine across the globe includes some meat dishes, although some have cultural or religious constraints about eating particular animals. In the West, meat constitutes a major part of the diet and tender, distinctive cuts, such as steaks and chops, are generally more highly prized than the cheaper cuts that require long, slow cooking to render them edible.

For many people, a meal that doesn't include such recognizable cuts of meat simply isn't a proper meal. Others, who eat meat occasionally rather than every day, like their carnivorous option to be a bit of a treat, something that

they can "get their teeth into"– roast lamb or sirloin steak, for example. It's human nature to push the boat out when entertaining guests or cooking for special occasions and celebrations, so we tend to buy more luxurious ingredients and that includes the best cuts of meat, such as tenderloin of beef. After all, why miss the opportunity to indulge in Festive Beef Wellington (see page 160) even if you have to live on sausages and pasta for the rest of the month?

Of course, not all these cuts will break the family budget. Pork, for example, is usually quite an economical buy, whether chops for broiling, a leg or a piece of cured ham for roasting, or ham steaks for frying. Although it may be more difficult to carve, many people consider shoulder of lamb to have the sweetest and most tender meat yet it is a much less expensive cut than leg. No barbecue will ever be complete without a rack of ribs, a wonderfully inexpensive and messy delight.

This book is packed with recipes for cooking steaks, chops, roasts, and ribs of all kinds – from veal to venison – and offers useful advice and guidance on buying, storing, and handling meat. And, to make the meal complete, the final chapter provides some great ideas for side dishes to serve as accompaniments.

NUTRITION

In recent years, red meat has had a bad press and its consumption has been blamed for a wide variety of medical conditions, some of them life-threatening. This is simplistic and not really justified, as these problems are generally caused by over-indulgence – eating any food to excess, even carrots, can cause health problems. Cooking techniques also have a role to play in the healthy diet. Grilled or broiled chops are certainly healthier options than pan-fried and it is also sensible to give some thought to accompaniments. Steak and French fries may be a classic combination, but it's the latter that really increases the unhealthy fat content of the meal. Once in a while is fine, but there are lots of other tasty possibilities.

Meat is a valuable source of protein and what's more it's high quality protein that contains the essential eight amino acids, which the human body cannot synthesize itself. Protein is vital for good health and plays an important role in the growth, maintenance, and repair of the body's cells. As an approximate guide, the protein content of broiled, grilled, or roasted lean cuts is as follows:

3¹/₂ oz/100 g beef	1-1¹/₈ oz/27–29 g protein
3¹/₂ oz/100 g lamb	³/₄-1¹/₈ oz/23–29 g protein
3¹/₂ oz/100 g pork	1-1¹/₄ oz/26–30 g protein
3¹/₂ oz/100 g veal	1¹/₄ oz/31 g protein
3¹/₂ oz/100 g venison	1³/₈ oz/35 g protein

The body requires relatively small amounts of protein and nutritionists recommend that protein-rich foods should constitute only 12 percent of the daily diet. In effect, this means 2 oz/55 g for adult men, 1½ oz/40 g for adult women, and 1⅛ oz/28 g for children aged between seven and ten.

Most people are now aware that a diet high in fats, especially saturated fat, is the cause of many health problems, from obesity to heart disease. In the last fifty years, meat producers have bred animals that have become progressively leaner. Some meats now contain less than half the fat that was typical in the 1950s and even pork, which was once considered excessively fatty, now sometimes needs basting during cooking to prevent it from drying out. As an approximate guide, the fat content of broiled, grilled, or roasted lean cuts is as follows:

3¹/₂ oz/100 g beef	¹/₈–¹/₂ oz/4–12 g fat
3¹/₂ oz/100 g lamb	³/₁₀–¹/₂ oz/8–12 g fat
3¹/₂ oz/100g pork	¹/₅–¹/₂ oz/6–10 g fat
3¹/₂ oz/100 g veal	¹/₂ oz/12 g fat
3¹/₂ oz/100 g venison	¹/₅ oz/6 g fat

Some fat – about 1 oz/25 g – is necessary in the diet. Most of the fat in meat is saturated and nutritionists recommend that this should make up no more than 10 percent of an adult's daily intake of calories. This is because these fats increase the level of blood cholesterol which can lead to medical conditions such as heart disease. Cholesterol present in food is not thought to have any effect on blood cholesterol levels.

Meat does not contain dietary fiber or carbohydrates. However, it is a source of some important minerals and vitamins – iron, zinc, magnesium, niacin, riboflavin (vitamin B2), thiamine (vitamin B1), and vitamin B12.

Buying meat

Whatever type of meat you are buying, it is important to select the right cut for the cooking method and recipe you have chosen. Suitable cuts for roasting, broiling, grilling, and frying are the ones that come from the back of the animal where the muscles have had to do the least amount of work – the saddle, loin, and tenderloin, for example. Legs and shoulders may also be roasted.

Meat should always smell pleasant and look attractive. The surface should be slightly moist, but not damp or slimy. So-called white meat should be pinkish in color, while red meat, particularly beef, should be dark red rather than crimson. Very young veal is pinkish-gray in color. Any fat should be fairly soft in texture and white or creamy colored, not yellow.

Beef: Although it is tempting to buy small, neat, boneless cuts, such as top rump for roasting because they look attractive and are easy to carve, these are best kept for pot-roasting. The best roasting cuts are from the ribs, tenderloin, back, and sirloin. Both fore rib and middle rib are available boned and rolled, but prime rib is usually sold on the bone and is regarded as one of the best roasting cuts. Rolled ribs are easier to carve, but standing ribs look more impressive.

For frying, grilling, and broiling, buy tender steaks such as fillet, sirloin, porterhouse, T-bone, Delmonico, entrecôte, and round. Flank steak, sometimes known as London broil, varies in tenderness but can be an economical choice.

Lamb: Unlike beef, which is taken from a mature animal, lamb comes from animals of less than a year old, usually about six to seven months. This results in tender meat and smaller cuts. Interestingly, there is currently a movement toward reinstating that nineteenth-century favorite, mutton, which comes from the mature sheep. Older lamb, known as hogget, is popular in some parts of the world, particularly Australia and New Zealand.

Several cuts are suitable for roasting. The leg, weighing 4–6 lb/1.8–2.7 kg, is a popular choice. It is also commonly sold divided into two pieces – the knuckle or shank and the sirloin leg roast – and is available in various other forms, including American leg roast, French leg roast, and center leg roast. Rack of lamb, also known as cross rib, is an economical cut for roasting, ideal for serving two or three people. It is also used to make a guard of honor – two racks placed, fat side out, facing each other with the ribs interlocked – and crown roast – two racks formed into a round, fat side facing in, with the central cavity filled with stuffing. Both of these look very appetizing and are a good choice for entertaining. The saddle or loin is extremely tender and is the most expensive cut. Weighing up to 8 lb/3.6 kg, it is a magnificent and impressive cut for entertaining. Smaller cuts from the loin are also suitable for roasting and these may be boned and rolled. Shoulder and half shoulder are quite fatty cuts but the meat is very sweet.

There are several kinds of chops, including sirloin, loin, and rib chops. Lamb steaks are usually taken from the leg sirloin.

Pork: Like lamb, pork comes from the young animal, so the meat is tender and there is a wide choice of quality cuts. As the ham is so big, it is usually cut into two pieces, both of which may be roasted. Similarly, the loin is usually divided into the hind or rear and fore or front loin, but the whole loin, weighing up to 12 lb/5.5 kg may be roasted if you are entertaining a large number of guests. The tenderloin, also known as pork fillet, may be roasted or pan-fried.

Chops are cut from the loin and may include loin, sirloin, and top loin States. Rib chops, taken from the shoulder, are not so tender as those from the loin, but are succulent and less expensive. Ribs or spare ribs are taken

from the side and are usually sold in sheets for cooking on the barbecue or in Chinese sauces.

Veal: Veal is very tender, offering a wide choice of cuts. The leg, loin, and rib may all be roasted and the shoulder is often boned and rolled for roasting. Chops, fillets, and scallops from the leg are usually pan-fried, but Florentine chops, the equivalent of the beef T-bone steak, can be broiled.

STORING AND HANDLING MEAT

Always store meat in the refrigerator – it is best placed on the bottom shelf to prevent any juices from dripping onto other foods and contaminating them. Keep raw meat completely separate from cooked foods. If it's pre-packed, as it is in many supermarkets, simply place the pack on a plate before putting in the refrigerator. Otherwise, wrap it in foil and place on a plate first. Beef, lamb, and mutton will keep for 3–5 days and pork and veal will keep for 2–4 days. Chops and steaks will go off more rapidly than roasts. Always observe the use-by date on the packaging.

To avoid cross-contamination, it is sensible to keep a cutting board specifically for meat and never use it for vegetables or other ingredients. Polyethylene is better than wood as it can be sterilized and is dishwasher safe. Wash your hands and any kitchen tools, such as knives, after handling raw meat before touching other raw or cooked ingredients.

MARINADES

Red Wine Marinade

Makes about ¾ cup
Preparation time: 5 minutes

⅔ cup full-bodied red wine
1 tbsp red wine vinegar
1 tbsp olive oil
2 garlic cloves, finely chopped
2 bay leaves, torn
pepper

Whisk together all the ingredients in a pitcher and season with pepper. Pour over red meat or venison, cover and leave to marinate for up to 12 hours.

White Wine Marinade

Makes about 1¼ cups
Preparation time: 5 minutes

1 cup dry white wine
6 tbsp olive oil
2 tbsp freshly squeezed lemon juice
3 tbsp finely chopped fresh flat-leaf parsley
1 tbsp snipped fresh chives
pepper

Whisk together all the ingredients in a pitcher and season with pepper. Pour over chops, cover, and leave to marinate for up to 12 hours.

Madeira Marinade

Makes generous 1 cup
Preparation time: 5 minutes, plus 30 minutes standing

6 tbsp freshly squeezed orange juice
¾ cup Madeira
4 shallots, finely chopped
grated rind of ½ orange
salt and pepper

Whisk together all the ingredients in a pitcher and season with salt and pepper. Leave to stand for 30 minutes to allow the flavors to mingle. Pour over any meat, cover, and leave to marinate for up to 12 hours.

Marinade with Juniper Berries

Makes 2¼ cups
Preparation time: 5 minutes

2¼ cups red wine
1 shallot, sliced
5 juniper berries, crushed
salt and pepper

Pour the wine into a shallow dish and add the onion and juniper berries. Season with salt and pepper and add pork or veal, turning to coat. Cover and leave to marinate for 5–12 hours, stirring occasionally.

1 STEAKS

Broiled, grilled, pan-fried, or cooked on a barbecue, steaks of all sorts are always popular but if served completely plain, they can be rather dull and unexciting. This chapter is packed with recipes for making the most of these tender cuts with marinades, salsas, relishes, and sauces to enhance their texture and flavor. Naturally, beef steaks take pride of place with a surprising variety of fabulous ways to cook them from Marinated Sirloin (see page 38) to Ginger Beef with Chili (see page 62). But there are lots of other choices too, including lamb, ham, pork, and even venison.

TABASCO STEAKS WITH
WATERCRESS BUTTER

1 BUNCH OF WATERCRESS

3 OZ/85 G UNSALTED BUTTER,
SOFTENED

4 SIRLOIN STEAKS,
ABOUT 8 OZ/225 G EACH

4 TSP TABASCO SAUCE

SALT AND PEPPER

SERVES 4

Preheat the barbecue. To make the watercress butter, using a
sharp knife, finely chop enough watercress to fill 4 tablespoons.
Set aside a few leaves for the garnish. Place the butter in a small
bowl and beat in the chopped watercress with a fork until fully
incorporated. Cover with plastic wrap and let chill in the
refrigerator until required.

Sprinkle each steak with 1 teaspoon of the Tabasco sauce, rubbing
it in well. Season to taste with salt and pepper.

Cook the steaks over hot coals for 2½ minutes each side for rare,
4 minutes each side for medium, and 6 minutes each side for
well done. Transfer to serving plates, garnish with the reserved
watercress leaves, and serve immediately, topped with the
watercress butter.

Alternative Cooking Method

A grill pan or skillet can also be used to cook this steak. Ensure
that you brush the pan with a little oil first and then pre-heat
before adding the meat. Cooking times may be increased slightly
as this method of cooking does not generate the high heat of a
barbecue. You therefore will need to look for visual signs that the
food is cooked to your liking.

SPICY LAMB STEAKS

4 LAMB STEAKS,
ABOUT 6 OZ/175 G EACH

8 FRESH ROSEMARY SPRIGS

8 FRESH BAY LEAVES

2 TBSP OLIVE OIL

SPICY MARINADE

2 TBSP CORN OIL

1 LARGE ONION, FINELY CHOPPED

2 GARLIC CLOVES, FINELY
CHOPPED

2 TBSP JAMAICAN JERK
SEASONING

1 TBSP CURRY PASTE

1 TSP GRATED FRESH GINGERROOT

14 OZ/400 G CANNED CHOPPED
TOMATOES

4 TBSP WORCESTERSHIRE SAUCE

3 TBSP LIGHT BROWN SUGAR

SALT AND PEPPER

SERVES 4

To make the marinade, heat the oil in a heavy-bottom pan. Add the onion and garlic and cook, stirring occasionally, for 5 minutes, or until softened. Stir in the jerk seasoning, curry paste, and grated ginger, and cook, stirring constantly, for 2 minutes. Add the tomatoes, Worcestershire sauce, and sugar, then season to taste with salt and pepper. Bring to a boil, stirring constantly, then reduce the heat and let simmer for 15 minutes, or until thickened. Remove from the heat and let cool.

Place the lamb steaks between 2 sheets of plastic wrap and beat with the side of a rolling pin to flatten. Transfer the steaks to a large, shallow, nonmetallic dish. Pour the marinade over them, turning to coat. Cover with plastic wrap and let marinate in the refrigerator for 3 hours.

Preheat the barbecue. Drain the lamb, reserving the marinade. Cook the lamb over medium hot coals, brushing frequently with the marinade, for 5–7 minutes on each side. Meanwhile, dip the rosemary and bay leaves in the olive oil and cook on the barbecue for 3–5 minutes. Serve the lamb immediately with the herbs.

Alternative Cooking Method

A grill pan or skillet can also be used to cook this steak. Ensure that you brush the pan with a little oil first and then pre-heat before adding the meat. Cooking times may be increased slightly as this method of cooking does not generate the high heat of a barbecue. You therefore will need to look for visual signs that the food is cooked to your liking.

GRILLED STEAK WITH HOT CHILI SALSA

4 SIRLOIN STEAKS,
ABOUT 8 OZ/225 G EACH
CORN OIL, FOR BRUSHING
SALT AND PEPPER

FOR THE SALSA
4 FRESH RED HABANERO OR
SCOTCH BONNET CHILIES
4 FRESH GREEN POBLANO CHILIES
3 TOMATOES, PEELED,
SEEDED, AND DICED
2 TBSP CHOPPED FRESH CILANTRO
1 TBSP RED WINE VINEGAR
2 TBSP OLIVE OIL

SERVES 4

First make the salsa. Preheat the broiler. Arrange the chilies on a baking sheet and cook, turning frequently, until blackened and charred. Let cool, then rub off the skins with paper towels. Halve and seed the chilies, then chop finely.

Mix the red and green chilies, tomatoes, and cilantro together in a bowl. Blend the vinegar and oil together in a pitcher, season with salt, and pour over the salsa. Toss well, cover, and let chill in the refrigerator until required.

Season the steaks with salt and pepper. Brush a grill pan or electric grill lightly with oil and heat over medium heat until hot. Cook the steaks for 2–4 minutes on each side, or until cooked to your liking. Serve at once with the salsa.

GLAZED HAM
STEAKS

4 CURED HAM STEAKS

4 TBSP DARK BROWN SUGAR

2 TSP MUSTARD POWDER

4 TBSP BUTTER

8 SLICES PINEAPPLE

TO SERVE

BAKED POTATOES AND

GREEN BEANS

SERVES 4

Preheat the ridged skillet over medium heat, place the ham steaks on it, and cook for 5 minutes, turning once. If you have room for only 2 steaks at a time, cook them completely and keep warm while cooking the second pair.

Combine the brown sugar and mustard in a small bowl.

Melt the butter in a large skillet, add the pineapple, and cook for 2 minutes to heat through, turning once. Sprinkle with the sugar and mustard and continue cooking over low heat until the sugar has melted and the pineapple is well glazed. Turn the pineapple once more so that both sides are coated with sauce.

Place the ham steaks on individual plates and arrange 2 pineapple slices either next to them or overlapping on top. Spoon over some of the sweet pan juices.

Serve with baked potatoes and green beans.

MEXICAN STEAK WITH AVOCADO SALSA

4 BEEF STEAKS

3 TBSP CORN OIL,
PLUS EXTRA FOR OILING

½ RED ONION, GRATED

1 FRESH RED CHILI,
SEEDED AND FINELY CHOPPED

1 GARLIC CLOVE, CRUSHED

1 TBSP CHOPPED FRESH CILANTRO

½ TSP DRIED OREGANO

1 TSP GROUND CUMIN

AVOCADO SALSA

1 RIPE AVOCADO

GRATED RIND AND JUICE OF 1 LIME

1 TBSP CORN OIL

½ RED ONION, FINELY CHOPPED

1 FRESH RED CHILI,
SEEDED AND FINELY CHOPPED

1 TBSP CHOPPED FRESH CILANTRO

SALT AND PEPPER

SERVES 4

Using a sharp knife, make a few cuts in the edge of fat around each steak. Place the meat in a shallow, nonmetallic dish.

Mix the corn oil, onion, chili, garlic, cilantro, oregano, and cumin together in a small bowl. Pour the marinade over the steaks, turning the meat so that it is well coated. Cover and let marinate in the refrigerator for 1–2 hours.

Preheat the barbecue. To make the salsa, cut the avocado in half and remove the pit. Peel and cut the flesh into small dice. Place the avocado, lime rind and juice, corn oil, onion, chili, cilantro, and salt and pepper to taste in a bowl and mix well. Cover and let chill in the refrigerator until required.

Cook the steaks on an oiled rack over hot coals for 6–12 minutes on each side. Serve the steaks accompanied with the avocado salsa.

Alternative Cooking Method

A grill pan or skillet can also be used to cook this steak. Ensure that you brush the pan with a little oil first and then pre-heat before adding the meat. Cooking times may be increased slightly as this method of cooking does not generate the high heat of a barbecue. You therefore will need to look for visual signs that the food is cooked to your liking.

PORK STEAKS WITH LEMON-GRASS

MARINADE

2 GARLIC CLOVES, CRUSHED

½ TSP FRESHLY GROUND BLACK PEPPER

1 TBSP SUGAR

2 TBSP FISH SAUCE

2 TBSP SOY SAUCE

1 TBSP SESAME OIL

1 TBSP LIME JUICE

2 LEMON-GRASS STALKS, OUTER LEAVES REMOVED, CHOPPED FINELY

4 SPRING ONIONS, CHOPPED FINELY

2 TBSP COCONUT MILK

4 PORK STEAKS

TO GARNISH

LIME WEDGES

TO SERVE

SALAD AND STIR-FRIED VEGETABLES

SERVES 4

To make the marinade, place the garlic, pepper, sugar, fish sauce, soy sauce, sesame oil, lime juice, lemon-grass, scallions and coconut milk in a large shallow dish and mix well to combine.

Turn the pork steaks in the marinade, then cover the dish with plastic wrap and place in the refrigerator for 1 hour.

Broil the pork steaks under a preheated broiler or barbecue them over charcoal, for 5 minutes on each side, or until cooked through. Garnish with lime wedges and serve with salad or stir-fried vegetables.

STEAKS IN ORANGE SAUCE

2 LARGE ORANGES

1 OZ/25 G BUTTER

4 FILLET STEAKS,
ABOUT 6 OZ/175 G EACH

6 TBSP BEEF BOUILLON

1 TBSP BALSAMIC VINEGAR

SALT AND FRESHLY GROUND
BLACK PEPPER

TO GARNISH

SPRIGS OF FRESH PARSLEY

SERVES 4

Cut the oranges in half, then cut off 4 thin slices and reserve for the garnish. Squeeze the juice from the remaining orange halves.

Melt the butter in a heavy-bottomed skillet. Add the steaks and cook for 1–2 minutes on each side, or until browned and seared. Remove from the pan, season to taste with salt and pepper, set aside, and keep warm.

Pour the orange juice into the pan and add the beef bouillon and vinegar. Simmer over low heat for 2 minutes. Season the orange sauce to taste with salt and pepper and return the steaks to the pan. Heat through gently for about 2 minutes, or according to taste. Serve immediately, garnished with the reserved orange slices and the parsley.

BEEF WITH EXOTIC MUSHROOMS

4 BEEF STEAKS

1¾ OZ/50 G BUTTER

1–2 GARLIC CLOVES, CRUSHED

5½ OZ/150 G MIXED
EXOTIC MUSHROOMS

2 TBSP CHOPPED FRESH PARSLEY

TO SERVE

SALAD GREENS

CHERRY TOMATOES, HALVED

SERVES 4

Preheat the barbecue. Place the steaks on to a cutting board and using a sharp knife, cut a pocket into the side of each steak.

To make the stuffing, heat the butter in a large skillet. Add the garlic and cook gently for 1 minute. Add the mushrooms to the skillet and cook gently for 4–6 minutes, or until tender. Remove the skillet from the heat and stir in the parsley.

Divide the mushroom mixture into 4 and insert a portion into the pocket of each steak. Seal the pocket with a toothpick. If preparing ahead, allow the mixture to cool before stuffing the steaks.

Cook the steaks over hot coals, searing the meat over the hottest part of the grill for 2 minutes on each side. Move the steaks to an area with slightly less intense heat and cook for an additional 4–10 minutes on each side, depending on how well done you like your steaks.

Transfer the steaks to serving plates and remove the toothpicks. Serve the steaks with salad greens and cherry tomatoes.

Alternative Cooking Method

A grill pan or skillet can also be used to cook this steak. Ensure that you brush the pan with a little oil first and then pre-heat before adding the meat. Cooking times may be increased slightly as this method of cooking does not generate the high heat of a barbecue. You therefore will need to look for visual signs that the food is cooked to your liking.

PEPPER STEAK

2 TBSP BLACK OR
MIXED DRIED PEPPERCORNS,
COARSELY CRUSHED
4 FILLETS STEAKS,
ABOUT 1 INCH/2.5 CM THICK,
AT ROOM TEMPERATURE
⅛ STICK BUTTER
1 TSP SUNFLOWER-SEED OIL
4 TBSP BRANDY
4 TBSP CRÈME FRAÎCHE OR
HEAVY CREAM (OPTIONAL)
SALT AND PEPPER

TO GARNISH
WATERCRESS LEAVES

SERVES 4

Spread out the crushed peppercorns on a plate and press the steaks into them to coat on both sides.

Melt the butter with the oil in a large sauté pan or skillet over medium-high heat. Add the steaks in a single layer and cook for 3 minutes on each side for rare; 3½ minutes on each side for medium-rare; 4 minutes on each side for medium; and 4½–5 minutes on each side for well-done.

Transfer the steaks to a warmed plate and set aside, covering with foil to keep warm. Pour the brandy into the pan to deglaze, then increase the heat and use a wooden spoon to scrape any sediment from the bottom of the pan. Continue boiling until reduced to around 2 tablespoons.

Stir in any accumulated juices from the steaks. Spoon in the crème fraîche, if using, and continue boiling until the sauce is reduced by half again. Taste, and adjust the seasoning if necessary. Spoon the pan sauce over the steaks, then garnish with the watercress and serve at once.

NEAPOLITAN PORK STEAKS

4 PORK LOIN STEAKS,
EACH ABOUT 4½ OZ/125 G

SERVES 4

SAUCE
2 TBSP OLIVE OIL
1 GARLIC CLOVE, CHOPPED
1 LARGE ONION, SLICED
14 OZ/400 G CANNED TOMATOES
2 TSP YEAST EXTRACT
2¾ OZ/75 G BLACK OLIVES, PITTED
2 TBSP SHREDDED FRESH BASIL

TO GARNISH
FRESH BASIL LEAVES, FRESHLY
GRATED PARMESAN CHEESE

TO SERVE
FRESHLY COOKED VEGETABLES
AND FRESH ITALIAN BREAD

Heat the oil in a large skillet. Add the garlic and onion and cook, stirring, for 3–4 minutes, or until they just begin to soften.

Add the canned tomatoes and yeast extract to the skillet and simmer for about 5 minutes, or until the sauce starts to thicken.

Cook the pork steaks under a preheated broiler for 5 minutes on both sides, until the meat is cooked through. Set the pork aside and keep warm.

Add the olives and fresh shredded basil to the sauce in the skillet and stir quickly to combine.

Transfer the steaks to warm serving plates. Top the steaks with the sauce, sprinkle with freshly grated Parmesan cheese, and serve with cooked vegetables.

NEW ORLEANS STEAK
SANDWICH

4 TBSP OLIVE OIL

2 LARGE ONIONS,
SLICED THINLY INTO RINGS

2 GARLIC CLOVES, CHOPPED

1 TBSP RED WINE VINEGAR

1 TBSP CHOPPED FRESH THYME

3 TBSP CHOPPED FRESH PARSLEY

2 TSP PREPARED MILD MUSTARD

SALT AND PEPPER

4 RUMP STEAKS,
ABOUT 6 OZ/175 G EACH

8 SLICES SOURDOUGH OR
CRUSTY BREAD

4 OZ/115 G ROQUEFORT CHEESE,
CRUMBLED

4 TOMATOES, SLICED

1 BOSTON LETTUCE, SHREDDED

SERVES 4

Heat half the oil in a heavy-bottom skillet. Add the onions
and garlic, sprinkle with a pinch of salt, then cover and cook
over very low heat for 25–30 minutes, or until very soft and
caramelized.

Process the onion mixture in a food processor until smooth.
Scrape into a bowl, stir in the vinegar, thyme, parsley, and
mustard and season with salt and pepper. Cover and place at the
side of the barbecue.

Brush the steaks with the remaining oil and season with salt and
pepper. Grill on a hot barbecue for 2 minutes on each side for
rare, 4 minutes on each side for medium, or 6 minutes on each
side for well done.

Meanwhile, toast the bread on both sides. Spread the onion
mixture on the toast. Slice the steaks and top 4 toast slices with
the meat. Sprinkle with the crumbled Roquefort, then add the
tomatoes and lettuce leaves. Top with the remaining toast
and serve.

Alternative Cooking Method

A grill pan or skillet can also be used to cook this steak. Ensure
that you brush the pan with a little oil first and then pre-heat
before adding the meat. Cooking times may be increased slightly
as this method of cooking does not generate the high heat of a
barbecue. You therefore will need to look for visual signs that the
food is cooked to your liking.

PORK STEAKS WITH
MUSTARD AND APPLE

2 EATING APPLES, PEELED,
CORED, AND GRATED
1 CUP FRESH WHOLE-WHEAT
BREAD CRUMBS
1 TBSP CHOPPED FRESH SAGE
2 TSP WHOLE-GRAIN MUSTARD
4 PORK STEAKS
OLIVE OIL, FOR BRUSHING

TO GARNISH
WEDGES OF LEMON AND
SMALL SALAD

SERVES 4

Mix together the grated apples, bread crumbs, sage, and mustard
in a bowl. Trim any visible fat from the pork steaks and brush
with oil.

Grill the pork steaks over a medium barbecue for 6–7 minutes.
Remove the steaks from the barbecue, transfer to a board, and
turn them over. Press the topping firmly over them, then grill for
an additional 10–15 minutes.

Carefully transfer the steaks to serving plates, topping-side up,
garnish with lemon wedges and a small salad, and serve at once.

Alternative Cooking Method
A grill pan or skillet can also be used to cook this steak. Ensure
that you brush the pan with a little oil first and then pre-heat
before adding the meat. Cooking times may be increased slightly
as this method of cooking does not generate the high heat of a
barbecue. You therefore will need to look for visual signs that the
food is cooked to your liking.

MARINATED
SIRLOIN

6 SIRLOIN STEAKS,
ABOUT 6 OZ/175 G EACH

SERVES 6

MARINADE
¾ CUP GUINNESS
2 TBSP CORN OIL
3 TBSP BROWN SUGAR
2 TBSP WORCESTERSHIRE SAUCE
1 TBSP WHOLE-GRAIN MUSTARD
2 GARLIC CLOVES,
FINELY CHOPPED

MUSTARD BUTTER
8 OZ/225 G BUTTER, SOFTENED
2 TBSP TARRAGON MUSTARD
1 TBSP CHOPPED FRESH PARSLEY

Place the steaks in a large, shallow dish. Mix together the Guinness, corn oil, sugar, Worcestershire sauce, whole-grain mustard, and garlic in a pitcher. Pour the mixture over the steaks, turning to coat. Cover with plastic wrap and let marinate in the refrigerator for 4 hours.

Meanwhile, beat together the butter, mustard, and parsley in a bowl until combined. Cover and let chill until required.

Drain the steaks, reserving the marinade. Grill on a hot barbecue, brushing frequently with the marinade, for 2 minutes on each side for rare, 4 minutes on each side for medium, or 6 minutes on each side for well done. Serve at once, topped with the mustard butter.

Alternative Cooking Method
A grill pan or skillet can also be used to cook this steak. Ensure that you brush the pan with a little oil first and then pre-heat before adding the meat. Cooking times may be increased slightly as this method of cooking does not generate the high heat of a barbecue. You therefore will need to look for visual signs that the food is cooked to your liking.

CHARGRILLED VENISON STEAKS

4 VENISON STEAKS

MARINADE
⅓ CUP RED WINE
2 TBSP SUNFLOWER OIL
1 TBSP RED WINE VINEGAR
1 ONION, CHOPPED
FEW SPRIGS OF FRESH PARSLEY
2 SPRIGS OF FRESH THYME
1 BAY LEAF
1 TSP SUPERFINE SUGAR
½ TSP MILD MUSTARD
SALT AND PEPPER

TO SERVE
JACKET POTATOES, SALAD GREENS
AND CHERRY TOMATOES

VARIATION
FOR A VARIATION ON THIS
RED WINE MARINADE,
SEE PAGE 10

SERVES 4

Place the venison steaks in a shallow, nonmetallic dish.

Combine the wine, oil, wine vinegar, onion, fresh parsley,
thyme, bay leaf, sugar, mustard, and salt and pepper to taste in
a bowl or screw-top jar and stir or shake vigorously, until well
combined. Alternatively, using a fork, whisk the ingredients
together in a bowl.

Pour the marinade mixture over the venison, cover, and let
marinate in the refrigerator overnight. Turn the steaks over in
the mixture occasionally so that the meat is well coated.

Cook the venison over hot coals, searing the meat over the
hottest part of the grill for about 2 minutes on each side.

Move the meat to an area with slightly less intense heat and grill
for another 4–10 minutes on each side, depending on how well
done you like your steaks.

Serve with jacket potatoes, salad greens, and cherry tomatoes.

Alternative Cooking Method
A grill pan or skillet can also be used to cook this steak. Ensure
that you brush the pan with a little oil first and then pre-heat
before adding the meat. Cooking times may be increased slightly
as this method of cooking does not generate the high heat of a
barbecue. You therefore will need to look for visual signs that the
food is cooked to your liking.

MUSTARD STEAKS WITH TOMATO RELISH

4 SIRLOIN OR RUMP STEAKS

1 TBSP TARRAGON MUSTARD

2 GARLIC CLOVES, CRUSHED

TOMATO RELISH

2 CUPS CHERRY TOMATOES

2 TBSP BROWN SUGAR

¼ CUP WHITE WINE VINEGAR

1 PIECE OF PRESERVED GINGER, CHOPPED

½ LIME, THINLY SLICED

SALT

TO GARNISH

FRESH TARRAGON SPRIGS

SERVES 4

To make the tomato relish, place all the ingredients in a heavy bottom pan, seasoning to taste with salt. Bring to a boil, stirring until the sugar has completely dissolved. Reduce the heat and let simmer, stirring occasionally, for 40 minutes, or until thickened. Transfer to a bowl, cover with plastic wrap and let cool.

Preheat the barbecue. Using a sharp knife, cut almost completely through each steak horizontally to make a pocket. Spread the mustard inside the pockets and rub the steaks all over with the garlic. Place them on a plate, cover with plastic wrap and let stand for 30 minutes.

Cook the steaks over hot coals for 2½ minutes each side for rare, 4 minutes each side for medium, or 6 minutes each side for well done. Transfer to serving plates, garnish with fresh tarragon sprigs, and serve immediately with the tomato relish.

Alternative Cooking Method

A grill pan or skillet can also be used to cook this steak. Ensure that you brush the pan with a little oil first and then pre-heat before adding the meat. Cooking times may be increased slightly as this method of cooking does not generate the high heat of a barbecue. You therefore will need to look for visual signs that the food is cooked to your liking.

HAM STEAK IN MADEIRA SAUCE

4 HAM STEAKS,
ABOUT 8 OZ/225 G EACH
2 TBSP BUTTER
2 CLOVES
1 MACE BLADE
1 CUP MADEIRA
2 TSP MEAUX MUSTARD

TO GARNISH
FRESH FLAT-LEAF
PARSLEY SPRIGS

VARIATION
FOR A VARIATION ON THIS
MADEIRA SAUCE,
SEE PAGE 10

SERVES 4

Snip the edges of the ham steaks with kitchen scissors to prevent them from curling up as they cook.

Melt the butter in a large, heavy-bottom skillet, then add the cloves and mace blade. Add the ham, in batches if necessary, and cook for 3 minutes on each side. Transfer to a warmed dish, cover, and keep warm.

Add the Madeira to the skillet and bring to a boil, stirring and scraping up any sediment from the bottom of the skillet. Stir in the mustard and cook for 2 minutes, or until the sauce is thickened and glossy. Pour the sauce over the ham, garnish with parsley sprigs, and serve immediately.

TEQUILA-MARINATED BEEF STEAKS

2 TBSP OLIVE OIL
3 TBSP TEQUILA
3 TBSP FRESHLY SQUEEZED ORANGE JUICE
1 TBSP FRESHLY SQUEEZED LIME JUICE
3 GARLIC CLOVES, CRUSHED
2 TSP CHILI POWDER
2 TSP GROUND CUMIN
1 TSP DRIED OREGANO
SALT AND PEPPER
4 SIRLOIN STEAKS

SERVES 4

Place the oil, tequila, orange and lime juices, garlic, chili powder, cumin, oregano, and salt and pepper to taste in a large, shallow, nonmetallic dish and mix together. Add the steaks and turn to coat in the marinade. Cover and let chill in the refrigerator for at least 2 hours or overnight, turning occasionally.

Preheat the barbecue and oil the grill rack. Let the steaks return to room temperature, then remove from the marinade. Cook over hot coals for 3–4 minutes on each side for medium, or longer according to taste, basting frequently with the marinade. Serve at once.

Alternative Cooking Method

A grill pan or skillet can also be used to cook this steak. Ensure that you brush the pan with a little oil first and then pre-heat before adding the meat. Cooking times may be increased slightly as this method of cooking does not generate the high heat of a barbecue. You therefore will need to look for visual signs that the food is cooked to your liking.

RUMP STEAK WITH DARK
BARBECUE SAUCE

2 TBSP CORN OIL

MARINADE

1 ONION, FINELY CHOPPED

1 LB/450 G TOMATOES, PEELED,
SEEDED, AND CHOPPED

2 TBSP LEMON JUICE

1 TBSP TABASCO SAUCE

2 TBSP WORCESTERSHIRE SAUCE

2 TBSP BROWN SUGAR

1 TSP MUSTARD POWDER

5 OZ/140 G SHALLOTS,
FINELY CHOPPED

5 OZ/140 G BUTTER, SOFTENED

6 RUMP STEAKS,
ABOUT 6 OZ/175 G EACH

SALT AND PEPPER

TO GARNISH

FEW SPRIGS OF WATERCRESS

SERVES 6

Heat the oil in a large skillet. Cook the onion over low heat, stirring occasionally, for 5 minutes, or until softened. Stir in the tomatoes, lemon juice, Tabasco and Worcestershire sauces, sugar, and mustard powder. Cover and let simmer, stirring occasionally, for 15–20 minutes, or until thickened. Pour into a large dish and let cool.

Meanwhile, blanch the shallots in boiling water for 2–3 minutes. Drain well and pat dry with paper towels. Place in a food processor and process to a purée. Gradually work in the butter and season with salt and pepper. Scrape the shallot butter into a bowl, cover, and let chill until required.

Add the steaks to the cooled marinade, turning to coat. Cover and let marinate in a cool place for 4 hours.

Drain the steaks, reserving the marinade. Grill on a hot barbecue, brushing frequently with the marinade, for 2 minutes on each side for rare, 4 minutes on each side for medium, or 6 minutes on each side for well done. Serve each steak topped with a spoonful of shallot butter and garnish with watercress sprigs.

Alternative Cooking Method
A grill pan or skillet can also be used to cook this steak. Ensure that you brush the pan with a little oil first and then pre-heat before adding the meat. Cooking times may be increased slightly as this method of cooking does not generate the high heat of a barbecue. You therefore will need to look for visual signs that the food is cooked to your liking.

STEAK WITH COUNTRY GRAVY

4 ROUND STEAKS,
ABOUT 5 OZ/140 G EACH
1 CUP ALL-PURPOSE FLOUR
PINCH OF CAYENNE PEPPER,
OR TO TASTE
3–4 TBSP RENDERED BACON FAT
OR CORN OR PEANUT OIL
1¼ CUPS MILK OR LIGHT CREAM
SALT AND PEPPER

SERVES 4

Put the steaks between pieces of waxed paper and use a rolling pin to beat them until they are about ¼ inch/5 mm thick. Set aside.

Put the flour onto a large plate and season with cayenne pepper and salt and pepper to taste. Dust the steaks with the seasoned flour on both sides, shaking off any excess, and set aside the leftover flour.

Heat 3 tablespoons of the bacon fat in a large skillet over medium-high heat. Add as many steaks as will fit without overcrowding the skillet and cook for 5–6 minutes, turning once, until they are cooked through as desired and are crisp and brown on the outside. Transfer the steaks to a plate and keep warm in a low oven while cooking the remaining steaks, if necessary. Add more fat to the skillet as needed.

To make the country gravy, put 5 tablespoons of the reserved seasoned flour into a small bowl, slowly stir in half the milk, and continue stirring until no lumps remain.

Pour off all but about 1 tablespoon of the fat in the skillet. Pour the milk mixture into the skillet, stirring to scrape up the sediment. Pour in the remaining milk and bring to a boil. Reduce the heat and let simmer for 2 minutes, stirring constantly, to remove the raw flour taste. Taste and adjust the seasoning, if necessary. Serve the steaks with the gravy poured over.

BOOZY BEEF STEAKS

4 BEEF STEAKS
4 TBSP WHISKY OR BRANDY
2 TBSP SOY SAUCE
1 TBSP DARK BROWN SUGAR
PEPPER
TOMATO SLICES

TO GARNISH
FRESH PARSLEY SPRIGS

TO SERVE
GARLIC BREAD

SERVES 4

Make a few cuts in the edge of fat on each steak. This will stop the meat curling as it cooks. Place the meat in a shallow, nonmetallic dish.

Mix the whisky, soy sauce, sugar, and pepper to taste together in a small bowl, stirring until the sugar dissolves. Pour the mixture over the steak. Cover with plastic wrap and let marinate in the refrigerator for at least 2 hours. Preheat the barbecue. Cook the beef steaks over hot coals, searing the meat over the hottest part of the grill for 2 minutes on each side.

Move the meat to an area with slightly less intense heat and cook for an additional 4–10 minutes on each side, depending on how well done you like your steaks. To test if the meat is cooked, insert the point of a sharp knife into the meat – the juices will run from red when the meat is still rare, to clear as it becomes well cooked.

Lightly grill the tomato slices for 1–2 minutes. Transfer the meat and the tomatoes to warmed serving plates. Garnish with fresh parsley sprigs and serve with garlic bread.

Alternative Cooking Method
A grill pan or skillet can also be used to cook this steak and tomato dish. Ensure that you brush the pan with a little oil first and then pre-heat before adding the meat. Cooking times may be increased slightly as this method of cooking does not generate the high heat of a barbecue. You therefore will need to look for visual signs that the food is cooked to your liking.

STEAK WITH BLUE CHEES
TOPPING

MARINADE

⅔ CUP RED WINE

1 TBSP RED WINE VINEGAR

1 TBSP OLIVE OIL

1 GARLIC CLOVE, FINELY CHOPPED

1 BAY LEAF, CRUMBLED

1 TBSP WHOLE-GRAIN MUSTARD

4 RUMP OR SIRLOIN STEAKS,
ABOUT 6 OZ/175 G EACH

2 OZ/55 G BLUE CHEESE,
SUCH AS GORGONZOLA

1 CUP FRESH WHITE
BREADCRUMBS

2 TBSP CHOPPED FRESH PARSLEY

TO GARNISH

A SMALL SALAD

SERVES 4

Mix together the red wine, vinegar, olive oil, garlic, bay leaf, and mustard in a shallow dish. Add the steaks, turning to coat, then cover and let stand in a cool place to marinate for 4 hours.

Meanwhile, mix together the blue cheese, bread crumbs, and parsley in a small bowl. Cover and store in the refrigerator until required.

Drain the steaks. Grill on an indoor grill or in a grill pan for 2 minutes on each side for rare, 4 minutes on each side for medium, or 6 minutes on each side for well done. Spoon the cheese topping onto the steaks, pressing it down with the back of the spoon, when you turn the steaks. Serve at once, garnished with a small salad.

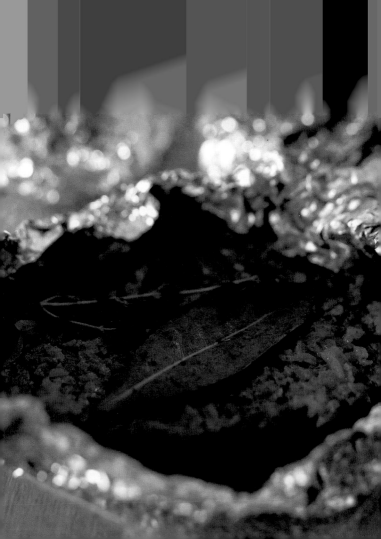

STEAK PACKAGES

4 SIRLOIN OR RUMP STEAKS

1¼ CUPS DRY RED WINE

2 TBSP OLIVE OIL

SALT AND PEPPER

1 OZ/25 G BUTTER

2 TSP DIJON MUSTARD

4 SHALLOTS, FINELY CHOPPED

4 FRESH THYME SPRIGS

4 BAY LEAVES

VARIATION

FOR A VARIATION ON THIS
RED WINE MARINADE,
SEE PAGE 10

SERVES 4

Place the steaks in a large, shallow, nonmetallic dish. Mix the wine and oil together in a measuring cup and season to taste with salt and pepper. Pour the marinade over the steaks, cover with plastic wrap, and let marinate in the refrigerator for up to 8 hours.

Preheat the barbecue. Cut out 4 squares of foil large enough to enclose the steaks and coat the centers with the butter and mustard. Drain the steaks and place them on the foil squares. Top with the shallots, thyme, and bay leaves and fold over the foil to make neat packages.

Cook the packages over hot coals for 10 minutes, turning once. Serve the steaks immediately in the packages.

Alternative Cooking Method

Preheat the oven to 350°F / 180°C. Cook the steaks in their packages for 15-20 mins, checking after 10 mins to see if the steak is cooked to your liking.

PORK IN WHITE WINE AND
OLIVE SAUCE

1 TSP OLIVE OIL
1 BONELESS PORK STEAK
¼ TSP DRIED OREGANO
¼ TSP DRIED THYME
SALT AND PEPPER
2 TSP LEMON JUICE
4 TBSP DRY WHITE WINE
4 TBSP WATER
6 BLACK OLIVES

TO SERVE
RICE OR FRESH PASTA

VARIATION
FOR A VARIATION ON THIS
WHITE WINE SAUCE,
SEE PAGE 10

SERVES 1

Sprinkle oil over the pork steak. Rub in the herbs and salt and pepper to season.

Heat a nonstick skillet and brown the pork quickly over high heat, turning once.

Pour in the lemon juice, wine, and water. Bring to a boil, then reduce the heat, cover, and simmer gently for 15 minutes.

Add the olives to the skillet and continue cooking for 5 minutes more to heat through.

Serve with rice or fresh pasta.

BEEF WITH BELL PEPPER
AND TOMATOES

2 TBSP ALL-PURPOSE FLOUR

SALT AND PEPPER

1 VERY THIN DELMONICO OR

SIRLOIN STEAK

1 TBSP OLIVE OIL

1 TBSP SWEET BUTTER

SAUCE

½ SMALL RED BELL PEPPER, DICED

2 TOMATOES, PEELED AND DICED

¼ CUP DRY WHITE WINE

2 TBSP LEMON JUICE

SERVES 1

Season the flour with salt and pepper. Dredge the steak in the flour, shaking off any excess.

Heat the oil over high heat in a large skillet. When it is sizzling, add the butter, and cook until melted. Swirl the skillet around to combine the oil and butter.

Cook the steak in the skillet over high heat for 1–2 minutes depending on the thickness, then turn, and cook the other side for 1–2 minutes. The meat should not be too rare for this dish.

Transfer the cooked steak to a warm serving dish. Scrape the bottom of the skillet with a wooden spoon to incorporate any sediment that has stuck to the bottom.

Add the diced bell pepper and tomatoes to the skillet and mix well. Stir in the wine and lemon juice. Bring to a boil, reduce the heat, and simmer for 2 minutes. Pour over the steak and serve.

GINGER BEEF WITH CHILI

4 LEAN BEEF STEAKS, SUCH AS
ROUND, SHORT LOIN OR
TENDERLOIN, 3½ OZ/100 G EACH
2 TBSP GINGER WINE
1 INCH/2.5 CM PIECE OF FRESH
GINGERROOT, FINELY CHOPPED
1 GARLIC CLOVE, CRUSHED
1 TSP GROUND CHILI
1 TSP VEGETABLE OIL
SALT AND PEPPER

RELISH

8 OZ/225 G FRESH PINEAPPLE
1 SMALL RED BELL PEPPER
1 FRESH RED CHILI
2 TBSP LIGHT SOY SAUCE
1 PIECE OF PRESERVED GINGER IN
SYRUP, DRAINED AND CHOPPED

TO GARNISH

FRESH RED CHILI STRIPS

TO SERVE

FRESHLY COOKED NOODLES
2 SCALLIONS, SHREDDED

SERVES 4

Trim any excess fat from the steaks if necessary. Using a meat mallet or covered rolling pin, pound the steaks until they are ½ inch/1 cm thick. Season on both sides with salt and pepper to taste and place in a shallow dish.

Combine the ginger wine, fresh ginger root, garlic, and chili and pour over the meat. Cover with plastic wrap and chill for 30 minutes.

Meanwhile, make the relish. Peel and finely chop the pineapple and place it in a bowl. Halve, deseed, and finely chop the bell pepper and chili. Stir into the pineapple with the soy sauce and preserved ginger. Cover with plastic wrap and chill until required.

Brush a ridged skillet with the oil and heat until very hot. Drain the beef and add to the skillet, pressing down to seal. Lower the heat and cook for 5 minutes. Turn the steaks over and cook for a further 5 minutes.

Drain the steaks on paper towels and transfer to warmed serving plates. Garnish with chili strips and serve with noodles, scallions, and the relish.

STEAKS WITH RED ONION

4 RUMP STEAKS

2 TSP WHOLE-GRAIN MUSTARD

SALT AND PEPPER

2 TBSP CORN OIL

GRATED RIND AND

JUICE OF ½ ORANGE

RED ONION MARMALADE

2 TBSP OLIVE OIL

1 LB/450 G RED ONIONS,

CUT INTO RINGS

GENEROUS ¾ CUP RED WINE

RIND OF 1 ORANGE, GRATED

1 TBSP SUPERFINE SUGAR

SALT AND PEPPER

TO SERVE

BOILED NEW POTATOES

SERVES 4

Preheat the barbecue. To make the marmalade, place the olive oil and onions in a pan and cook gently for 5–10 minutes, until the onions are just softened and beginning to turn golden brown. Add the wine, orange rind, and sugar to the pan and simmer for 10–15 minutes, until the onions are tender and most of the liquid has evaporated. Let cool, then season the mixture to taste with salt and pepper.

Make a few cuts in the edge of fat around each steak to prevent the meat curling as it cooks. Using a knife, spread each steak with a little of the mustard and season with salt and pepper.

Mix the corn oil, orange juice and rind together in a small bowl, then use to baste the steaks occasionally during cooking.

Cook the steaks over hot coals, searing them over the hottest part of the grill for 2 minutes on each side, basting occasionally with the orange juice mixture.

Move the meat to an area with slightly less intense heat and cook, basting occasionally, for an additional 4–10 minutes on each side, depending on how well done you like your steaks. Transfer the steaks to plates and serve with the red onion marmalade and new potatoes.

Alternative Cooking Method

A grill pan or skillet can also be used to cook this steak. Ensure that you brush the pan with a little oil first and then pre-heat before adding the meat. Cooking times may be increased slightly as this method of cooking does not generate the high heat of a barbecue. You therefore will need to look for visual signs that the food is cooked to your liking.

2 CHOPS

The perfect choice for midweek meals, chops are wonderfully versatile and this chapter is full of quick and clever ways to make them really special. There are recipes for traditional favorites, such as Minted Lamb Chops (see page 84) and Honey Glazed Pork Chops (see page 108), as well as a range of dishes from countries as diverse as Spain, Greece, Italy, France, the Middle East, and the Caribbean. Why not ring the changes with Veal with Pickled Vegetables (see page 76), Persian Lamb Chops (see page 82), or Pork in Lemon Sauce (see page 112) and liven up the family menu?

NEAPOLITAN VEAL CUTLET
WITH MASCARPONE

⅛ CUP BUTTER

4 9-OUNCE VEAL CUTLETS, TRIMMED

1 LARGE ONION, SLICED

2 APPLES, PEELED, CORED, AND SLICED

6 OUNCES BUTTON MUSHROOMS

1 TBSP CHOPPED FRESH TARRAGON

8 BLACK PEPPERCORNS

1 TBSP SESAME SEEDS

14 OUNCES DRIED MARILLE

½ CUP EXTRA-VIRGIN OLIVE OIL

¾ CUP MASCARPONE CHEESE, BROKEN INTO SMALL PIECES

SALT AND PEPPER

2 LARGE BEEF TOMATOES, CUT IN HALF

LEAVES OF 1 FRESH BASIL SPRIG

SERVES 4

Melt 4 tbsp of the butter in a skillet and fry the veal for 5 minutes on each side. Transfer to a dish and keep warm.

Fry the onion and apples in the pan until lightly browned. Transfer to a dish, place the veal on top, and keep warm.

Fry the mushrooms, tarragon, and peppercorns in the remaining butter for 3 minutes. Sprinkle with the sesame seeds.

Bring a pan of salted water to a boil. Add the pasta and 1 tbsp of the oil and cook until tender. Drain and transfer to a serving plate.

Top the pasta with the mascarpone cheese and sprinkle with the remaining olive oil. Place the onions, apples and veal cutlets on top of the pasta. Spoon the mushrooms, peppercorns, and pan juices onto the cutlets, place the tomatoes and basil leaves around the edge, and place in a preheated oven at 300°F/150°C for 5 minutes. Season with salt and pepper to taste and serve immediately.

LAMB WITH ZUCCHINI
AND TOMATOES

4-8 LAMB CHOPS

PEPPER

2 TBSP OLIVE OIL

1 ONION, CHOPPED FINELY

1 GARLIC CLOVE, CHOPPED FINELY

4 TBSP OUZO (OPTIONAL)

14 OZ/400 G CANNED TOMATOES
IN JUICE

9 OZ/250 G ZUCCHINI, SLICED

2 TBSP CHOPPED FRESH THYME

SALT

SERVES 4

Season the lamb chops with pepper. Heat the oil in a large,
flameproof casserole dish or Dutch oven, add the onion and
garlic, and fry for 5 minutes, until softened. Add the lamb chops
and fry until browned on both sides.

Stir the ouzo into the saucepan, if using, then add the tomatoes
with their juice, the sugar, zucchini, thyme, and salt. Bring to the
boil and then simmer for 30–45 minutes, stirring occasionally
and turning the chops once during cooking, until the lamb and
zucchini are tender. If necessary, add a little water during cooking
if the sauce becomes too thick. Serve hot.

HERBED PORK CHOPS

4 PORK CHOPS

MARINADE

4 TBSP CORN OIL

2 TBSP LEMON JUICE

1 TBSP CHOPPED FRESH
MARJORAM

1 TBSP CHOPPED FRESH THYME

2 TABLESPOONS CHOPPED FRESH
PARSLEY

1 GARLIC CLOVE, FINELY CHOPPED

1 ONION, FINELY CHOPPED

SALT AND PEPPER

**BLUE CHEESE AND
WALNUT BUTTER**

2 OZ/55 G BUTTER

4 SCALLIONS, FINELY CHOPPED

5 OZ/140 G GORGONZOLA CHEESE,
CRUMBLED

2 TBSP FINELY CHOPPED WALNUTS

TO SERVE

A SMALL SALAD

SERVES 4

Trim the fat from the chops and place them in a dish. Whisk together the oil, lemon juice, marjoram, thyme, parsley, garlic, and onion in a bowl, then season with salt and pepper. Pour the marinade over the chops, turning to coat. Cover and let marinate in the refrigerator overnight.

To make the flavored butter, melt half the butter in a skillet, and cook the scallions over low heat, stirring frequently for a few minutes, until softened. Transfer to a bowl and mix in the remaining butter, the cheese, and walnuts. Form into a roll, then cover and let chill until required.

Drain the chops, reserving the marinade. Grill the chops on a hot barbecue for 5 minutes on each side, then grill over more medium coals or on a higher rack, turning and brushing occasionally with the reserved marinade, for about 10 minutes more on each side, or until cooked through and tender. Transfer to serving plates and top each chop with 1–2 slices of the cheese and walnut butter. Serve at once with a small salad.

Alternative Cooking Method

Cook under a hot broiler. Cooking times may vary slightly if you use this method so you will need to look for visual signs that the food is cooked to your liking.

LAMB WITH BAY AND LEMON

4 LAMB CHOPS

1 TBSP CORN OIL

1 TBSP BUTTER

⅔ CUP WHITE WINE

⅔ CUP LAMB OR
VEGETABLE STOCK

2 BAY LEAVES

PARED RIND OF 1 LEMON

SALT AND PEPPER

SERVES 4

Using a sharp knife, carefully remove the bone from each lamb chop, keeping the meat intact. Alternatively, ask the butcher to prepare the lamb noisettes for you.

Shape the meat into rounds and secure with a length of string.

Heat the oil and butter together in a large skillet until the mixture begins to froth.

Add the lamb noisettes to the skillet and cook for 2–3 minutes on each side, or until browned all over.

Remove the pan from the heat. Remove the meat, then drain off all of the excess fat and discard. Place the noisettes back in the pan.

Return the pan to the heat. Add the wine, stock, bay leaves, and lemon rind and cook for 20–25 minutes, or until the lamb is tender. Season the lamb and sauce to taste with a little salt and pepper.

Transfer to serving plates. Remove the string from each noisette and serve with the sauce.

VEAL WITH PICKLED VEGETABLES

VEGETABLES

FOR THE VEGETABLE ESCABECHE

⅔ CUP OLIVE OIL

4 SHALLOTS, SLICED

2 PINCHES OF SAFFRON THREADS

1 LB/450 G YOUNG CARROTS,
PEELED AND SLICED THINLY

8 OZ/225 G GREEN BEANS,
CHOPPED SMALL

8 OZ/225 G TINY CAULIFLOWER
FLORETS

3 TBSP WHITE WINE VINEGAR

1 TSP CORIANDER SEEDS,
CRUSHED

½ TSP BLACK PEPPERCORNS,
CRUSHED

1 BAY LEAF, TORN IN HALF

4 VEAL LOIN CHOPS,
ABOUT 8 OZ/225 G EACH AND
¾ INCH/2 CM THICK

SALT AND PEPPER

TO GARNISH

2 TBSP FINELY CHOPPED
FRESH CHIVES

TO SERVE

GARLIC-FLAVORED OLIVE OIL

SERVES 4

To make the vegetable escabeche, heat the oil in a skillet over medium heat. Add the shallots and saffron and cook for 5–7 minutes until the shallots start to caramelize. Add the carrots, beans, and cauliflower. Reduce the heat to very low, cover, and cook for 5–8 minutes until the vegetables are tender-crisp. Stir in the vinegar, coriander seeds, peppercorns, and bay leaf. Remove from the heat and let cool, unless you are serving the dish immediately.

When ready to cook, lightly drizzle the chops with more oil and season with salt and pepper to taste. Place under a preheated hot broiler, about 4 inches/10 cm from the source of the heat, and broil for 3 minutes. Turn the chops over and broil for an additional 2 minutes if you like them cooked medium.

Transfer the chops to individual plates and spoon a little of the escabeche on the side of each. Sprinkle the vegetables with the chives, and drizzle with a little of the flavored oil. Serve at once.

BUTTERFLY CHOPS WITH
RED CURRANT GLAZE

4 TBSP RED CURRANT JELLY

2 TBSP RASPBERRY VINEGAR

½ TSP DRIED ROSEMARY

1 GARLIC CLOVE, CRUSHED

1 TBSP CORN OIL,
PLUS EXTRA FOR BASTING

4 BUTTERFLY LAMB CHOPS OR
8 LOIN LAMB CHOPS

4 BABY EGGPLANTS

SERVES 4

Preheat the barbecue. To make the glaze, place the red currant jelly, vinegar, rosemary, garlic, and corn oil in a pan and heat, stirring occasionally, until the jelly melts and the ingredients are well blended.

Cook the chops over hot coals for 5 minutes on each side. Cut each eggplant in half and brush the cut sides liberally with corn oil. Cook alongside the lamb for 3–4 minutes on each side. Keep warm.

Brush glaze over the chops and barbecue the meat for an additional 5 minutes on each side, basting frequently, until the meat is cooked through. Keep the red currant glaze warm at the side of the grill.

Transfer the lamb and eggplants to warmed serving plates and pour over the remaining red currant glaze. Serve immediately.

Alternative Cooking Method
A grill pan or skillet can also be used to cook these lamb chops. Ensure that you brush the pan with a little oil first and then pre-heat before adding the meat. Cooking times may be increased slightly as this method of cooking does not generate the high heat of a barbecue. You therefore will need to look for visual signs that the food is cooked to your liking.

GIN AND JUNIPER
PORK

4 PORK CHOPS,
ABOUT 6 OZ/175 G EACH

¼ CUP DRY GIN

¾ CUP ORANGE JUICE

2 RED OR WHITE ONIONS,
CUT IN HALF

6 JUNIPER BERRIES,
LIGHTLY CRUSHED

THINLY PARED RIND OF 1 ORANGE

1 CINNAMON STICK

1 BAY LEAF

2 TSP FINELY CHOPPED
FRESH THYME

SALT AND PEPPER

VARIATION

FOR A VARIATION ON THIS
JUNIPER SAUCE,
SEE PAGE 10

SERVES 4

Place the pork chops in a large, shallow, nonmetallic dish. Pour in the gin and orange juice and add the onion halves. Add the juniper berries, orange rind, cinnamon stick, bay leaf, and thyme and, using a fork, stir well until the pork chops are well coated. Cover with plastic wrap and let marinate in the refrigerator for up to 8 hours.

Preheat the barbecue. Drain the pork chops and onions, reserving the marinade. Season the pork chops with salt and pepper and strain the marinade into a small measuring cup.

Cook the pork and onions over medium hot coals, brushing frequently with the reserved marinade, for 7–9 minutes on each side, or until thoroughly cooked. Transfer to a large serving plate and serve immediately.

Alternative Cooking Method

A grill pan or skillet can also be used to cook these chops. Ensure that you brush the pan with a little oil first and then pre-heat before adding the meat. Cooking times may be increased slightly as this method of cooking does not generate the high heat of a barbecue. You therefore will need to look for visual signs that the food is cooked to your liking.

PERSIAN LAMB
CHOPS

2 TBSP CHOPPED FRESH MINT

1 CUP LOWFAT NATURAL YOGURT

4 GARLIC CLOVES, CRUSHED

¼ TSP PEPPER

6 LEAN LAMB CHOPS

2 TBSP LEMON JUICE

TABBOULEH

9 OZ/250 G COUSCOUS

SCANT 2 CUPS BOILING WATER

2 TBSP OLIVE OIL

2 TBSP LEMON JUICE

½ ONION, CHOPPED FINELY

4 TOMATOES, CHOPPED

1 OZ/25 G FRESH CORIANDER, CHOPPED

2 TBSP CHOPPED FRESH MINT

SALT AND PEPPER

SERVES 4-6

For the marinade, combine the mint, yogurt, garlic and pepper.

Put the chops into a non-porous dish and rub all over with the lemon juice. Pour the marinade over the chops. Cover and marinate for 2–3 hours.

To make the tabbouleh, put the couscous into a heatproof bowl and pour over the boiling water. Leave for 5 minutes. Drain and put into a strainer. Steam over a pan of barely simmering water for 8 minutes. Toss in the oil and lemon juice. Add the onion, tomato and herbs. Season and set aside.

Cook the lamb over medium hot coals for 15 minutes, turning once. Serve with the tabbouleh.

Alternative Cooking Method

A grill pan or skillet can also be used to cook these lamb chops. Ensure that you brush the pan with a little oil first and then pre-heat before adding the meat. Cooking times may be increased slightly as this method of cooking does not generate the high heat of a barbecue. You therefore will need to look for visual signs that the food is cooked to your liking.

MINTED
LAMB CHOPS

6 CHUMP CHOPS,
ABOUT 6 OZ/175 G EACH
⅔ CUP STRAINED PLAIN YOGURT
2 GARLIC CLOVES,
FINELY CHOPPED
1 TSP GRATED FRESH GINGERROOT
¼ TSP CORIANDER SEEDS,
CRUSHED
SALT AND PEPPER
1 TBSP OLIVE OIL,
PLUS EXTRA FOR BRUSHING
1 TBSP ORANGE JUICE
1 TSP WALNUT OIL
2 TBSP CHOPPED FRESH MINT

SERVES 6

Place the chops in a large, shallow, nonmetallic bowl. Mix half the yogurt, the garlic, ginger, and coriander seeds together in a measuring cup and season to taste with salt and pepper. Spoon the mixture over the chops, turning to coat, then cover with plastic wrap and let marinate in the refrigerator for 2 hours, turning occasionally.

Preheat the barbecue. Place the remaining yogurt, the olive oil, orange juice, walnut oil, and mint in a small bowl and, using a hand-held whisk, whisk until thoroughly blended. Season to taste with salt and pepper. Cover the minted yogurt with plastic wrap and let chill in the refrigerator until ready to serve.

Drain the chops, scraping off the marinade. Brush with olive oil and cook over medium hot coals for 5–7 minutes on each side. Serve immediately with the minted yogurt.

Alternative Cooking Method

A grill pan or skillet can also be used to cook these chops. Ensure that you brush the pan with a little oil first and then pre-heat before adding the meat. Cooking times may be increased slightly as this method of cooking does not generate the high heat of a barbecue. You therefore will need to look for visual signs that the food is cooked to your liking.

ITALIAN MARINATED PORK CHOPS

4 PORK RIB CHOPS

4 FRESH SAGE LEAVES

2 TBSP SALTED CAPERS

2 GHERKINS, CHOPPED

MARINADE

4 TBSP DRY WHITE WINE

1 TBSP BROWN SUGAR

2 TBSP OLIVE OIL

1 TSP DIJON MUSTARD

TO GARNISH

A SMALL SALAD

TO SERVE

GARLIC BREAD

VARIATION

FOR A VARIATION ON THIS
WHITE WINE MARINADE,
SEE PAGE 10

SERVES 4

Trim any visible fat from the chops and place them in a large,
shallow dish. Top each with a sage leaf. Rub the salt off the capers
with your fingers and sprinkle them over the chops, together
with the gherkins.

Mix the wine, sugar, oil, and mustard together in a small bowl
and pour the mixture over the chops. Cover with plastic wrap
and let marinate in a cool place for about 2 hours.

Drain the chops, reserving the marinade. Grill the chops on a hot
barbecue for 5 minutes on each side, then grill over more medium
coals or on a higher rack, turning and brushing occasionally with
the reserved marinade, for about 10 minutes more on each side,
or until cooked through and tender. Serve at once with a small
salad and garlic bread if you like.

Alternative Cooking Method

A grill pan or skillet can also be used to cook this steak. Ensure
that you brush the pan with a little oil first and then pre-heat
before adding the meat. Cooking times may be increased slightly
as this method of cooking does not generate the high heat of a
barbecue. You therefore will need to look for visual signs that the
food is cooked to your liking.

ROAST TOMATO AND
LAMB PACKETS

1 TBSP VEGETABLE OIL

1 LARGE LAMB CHOP OR STEAK

4 CHERRY TOMATOES

1 GARLIC CLOVE, CRUSHED

2 TSP FRESH TORN OREGANO OR

CHOPPED ROSEMARY

SALT AND PEPPER

SERVES 1

Preheat the oven to 325°F/160°C.

Heat the oil over high heat in a heavy skillet and brown
the lamb chop or steak on both sides.

Cut a large square of aluminum foil. Drain the meat and place in
the center of the foil. Arrange the tomatoes and garlic on top of
the meat. Sprinkle with the torn oregano or chopped rosemary,
salt, and pepper. Fold the foil to seal the packet and transfer to
a cookie sheet.

Bake in the oven for 45 minutes, or until the meat is tender.

Open the packet carefully so that the steam can escape, then
transfer the meat and tomatoes to a serving dish. Spoon on
the juices from the meat.

STICKY PORK CHOPS

SAUCE

¼ CUP PLUM, HOISIN,
SWEET & SOUR, OR DUCK SAUCE
1 TSP DARK BROWN SUGAR
1 TBSP TOMATO KETCHUP
PINCH OF GARLIC POWDER
2 TBSP DARK SOY SAUCE
4 LEAN PORK CHOPS (OR STEAKS)

TO SERVE

COOKED RICE AND PEAS

SERVES 4

Preheat a ridged skillet pan over a high heat.

Combine the sauce of your choice, brown sugar, ketchup, garlic powder, and soy sauce in a small mixing bowl.

Arrange the pork chops in a single layer on a flat dish. Brush the tops with sauce, then place the chops, sauce side down, on the pan. Cook the chops for 5 minutes, pressing down occasionally to get dark grid marks.

Brush the upper side of the chops with sauce, turn, and continue cooking for 5 minutes, or until dark grid marks appear.

Reduce the heat to medium and, turning once, cook the chops for about 10 more minutes, or until they are firm and the juices run clear when pierced with a toothpick.

Transfer the chops to a large dish and serve immediately, with the rice and peas.

LAMB WITH
EGGPLANT

1 EGGPLANT

SALT AND PEPPER

4-8 LAMB CHOPS

3 TBSP OLIVE OIL

1 ONION, CHOPPED COARSELY

1 GARLIC CLOVE, CHOPPED FINELY

14 OZ/400 G CANNED CHOPPED
TOMATOES IN JUICE

PINCH OF SUGAR

16 BLACK OLIVES, PITTED AND
CHOPPED COARSELY

1 TSP CHOPPED FRESH HERBS
SUCH AS BASIL, FLAT-LEAF
PARSLEY, OR OREGANO

SERVES 4

Cut the eggplant into ¾-inch/2-cm cubes, put in a colander
standing over a large plate, and sprinkle each layer with salt.
Cover with a plate and place a heavy weight on top. Leave for
30 minutes.

Preheat the broiler. Rinse the eggplant slices under cold running
water, then pat dry with paper towels. Season the lamb chops
with pepper.

Place the lamb chops on the broiler pan and cook under medium
heat for 10–15 minutes until tender, turning once during the
cooking time.

Meanwhile, heat the olive oil in a saucepan, add the eggplant,
onion, and garlic, and fry for 10 minutes, until softened and starting
to brown. Add the tomatoes and their juice, the sugar, olives,
chopped herbs, salt, and pepper and simmer for 5–10 minutes.

To serve, spoon the sauce onto 4 warmed serving plates and top
with the lamb chops.

CARIBBEAN PORK

4 PORK LOIN CHOPS
4 TBSP DARK BROWN SUGAR
4 TBSP ORANGE OR
PINEAPPLE JUICE
2 TBSP JAMAICAN RUM
1 TBSP DRY UNSWEETENED
COCONUT
½ TSP GROUND CINNAMON

COCONUT RICE
GENEROUS 1 CUP BASMATI RICE
2 CUPS WATER
⅔ CUP COCONUT MILK
4 TBSP RAISINS
4 TBSP ROASTED PEANUTS OR
CASHEWS
SALT AND PEPPER
2 TBSP DRY UNSWEETENED
COCONUT, TOASTED

TO SERVE
MIXED SALAD LEAVES

SERVES 4

Trim any excess fat from the pork and place the chops in a shallow, nonmetallic dish. Mix the sugar, fruit juice, rum, coconut, and cinnamon together in a bowl, stirring until the sugar dissolves. Pour the mixture over the pork, cover, and let marinate in the refrigerator for 2 hours, or preferably overnight.

Preheat the barbecue. Remove the pork from the marinade, reserving the liquid for basting. Cook over hot coals for 15–20 minutes, basting with the marinade.

Meanwhile, make the coconut rice. Rinse the rice under cold running water, place it in a pan with the water and coconut milk and bring gently to a boil. Stir, cover, and reduce the heat. Simmer gently for 12 minutes, or until the rice is tender and the liquid has been absorbed. Fluff up with a fork.

Stir the raisins and nuts into the rice, season to taste with salt and pepper, and sprinkle with the dry unsweetened coconut. Transfer the pork and rice to warmed serving plates and serve immediately with mixed salad greens.

Alternative Cooking Method
A grill pan or skillet can also be used to cook these pork chops. Ensure that you brush the pan with a little oil first and then pre-heat before adding the meat. Cooking times may be increased slightly as this method of cooking does not generate the high heat of a barbecue. You therefore will need to look for visual signs that the food is cooked to your liking.

MARINATED
LAMB CHOPS

8 LAMB LOIN CHOPS

SERVES 4

MARINADE

2 TBSP EXTRA-VIRGIN OLIVE OIL

2 TBSP WORCESTERSHIRE SAUCE

2 TBSP LEMON JUICE

2 TBSP DRY GIN

1 GARLIC CLOVE, FINELY CHOPPED

SALT AND PEPPER

MUSTARD BUTTER

2 OZ/55 G UNSALTED BUTTER, SOFTENED

1½ TSP TARRAGON MUSTARD

1 TBSP CHOPPED FRESH PARSLEY

DASH OF LEMON JUICE

TO GARNISH

FRESH PARSLEY SPRIGS

TO SERVE

SALAD

Preheat the barbecue. Place the lamb chops in a large, shallow, nonmetallic dish. Mix all the ingredients for the marinade together in a measuring cup, seasoning to taste with salt and pepper. Pour the mixture over the chops and then turn them until they are well coated. Cover with plastic wrap and let marinate for 5 minutes.

To make the mustard butter, mix all the ingredients together in a small bowl, beating with a fork until well blended. Cover with plastic wrap and let chill in the refrigerator until required.

Drain the chops, reserving the marinade. Cook over medium hot coals, brushing frequently with the reserved marinade, for 5 minutes on each side. Transfer to serving plates, top with the mustard butter, and garnish with parsley sprigs. Serve immediately with salad.

Alternative Cooking Method

A grill pan or skillet can also be used to cook these chops. Ensure that you brush the pan with a little oil first and then pre-heat before adding the meat. Cooking times may be increased slightly as this method of cooking does not generate the high heat of a barbecue. You therefore will need to look for visual signs that the food is cooked to your liking.

VIRGINIAN
PORK CHOPS

2 TBSP CORN OIL
4 PORK CHOPS,
ABOUT 6 OZ/175 G EACH
2 TBSP WHITE WINE
1 ONION, CHOPPED
14½ OZ/415 G CANNED PEACH
HALVES IN NATURAL JUICE,
DRAINED
1 TBSP PINK OR GREEN
PEPPERCORNS
⅓ CUP CHICKEN STOCK
2–3 TSP BALSAMIC VINEGAR
SALT AND PEPPER

SERVES 4

Heat half the corn oil in a large, heavy-bottom skillet. Add the
chops and cook for 6 minutes on each side, or until browned and
cooked through. Transfer to a plate, cover, and keep warm. Pour
off any excess fat from the skillet and return to the heat. Add the
wine and cook, for 2 minutes, stirring and scraping up any
sediment from the bottom of the skillet. Pour the liquid over the
meat, re-cover, and keep warm.

Wipe out the skillet with paper towels and heat the remaining
corn oil. Add the onion and cook over low heat, stirring
occasionally, for 5 minutes, or until softened. Meanwhile, slice
the peach halves.

Add the peaches to the skillet and heat through for 1 minute. Stir
in the peppercorns, pour in the chicken stock, and bring to
simmering point. Return the chops and cooking juices to the
skillet and season to taste with vinegar, salt and pepper. Transfer
to warmed plates and serve immediately.

ITALIAN LAMB CHOPS

4 LAMB CHOPS OR 8 LAMB CUTLETS

4 TOMATOES, HALVED

SERVES 4

MARINADE

2 TSP DRIED OREGANO

JUICE OF ½ LEMON

2 TBSP EXTRA-VIRGIN OLIVE OIL

TO GARNISH

A FEW BASIL LEAVES

TO SERVE

COOKED LINGUINE OR
OTHER PASTA

Arrange the lamb in a single layer in a shallow dish. Sprinkle with oregano, lemon juice, and oil. Cover the dish with plastic wrap and refrigerate overnight or for as long as possible.

About 10 minutes before cooking, remove the lamb from the refrigerator. Meanwhile, preheat a ridged skillet pan over a high heat.

Place the lamb in the hot skillet pan and sear for 2 minutes on each side. Reduce the heat and cook over medium heat for about 5 minutes longer, turning the pieces over once. If the chops are thick, you may need to allow a few extra minutes. The meat is best when it is pink inside.

About 2–3 minutes before the meat is ready, cook the tomato pieces on the griddle. Arrange the chops and cooked tomatoes on a large platter and serve immediately with the pasta, garnished with basil leaves.

PORK CHOPS WITH
SAGE

2 TBSP FLOUR

1 TBSP CHOPPED FRESH SAGE OR
1 TSP DRIED

4 LEAN BONELESS PORK CHOPS,
TRIMMED OF EXCESS FAT

2 TBSP OLIVE OIL

½ OZ/15 G BUTTER

2 RED ONIONS, SLICED INTO RINGS

1 TBSP LEMON JUICE

2 TSP SUPERFINE SUGAR

4 PLUM TOMATOES, QUARTERED

SALT AND PEPPER

TO SERVE

A GREEN SALAD

SERVES 4

Mix the flour, sage and salt and pepper to taste on a plate. Lightly dust the pork chops on both sides with the seasoned flour.

Heat the oil and butter in a skillet, add the chops and cook them for 6–7 minutes on each side until cooked through. Drain the chops, reserving the pan juices, and keep warm.

Toss the onion in the lemon juice and cook along with the sugar and tomatoes for 5 minutes until tender.

Serve the pork with the tomato and onion mixture and a green salad.

PORK WITH ORANGE SAUCE

4 TBSP FRESHLY SQUEEZED
ORANGE JUICE
4 TBSP RED WINE VINEGAR
2 GARLIC CLOVES,
FINELY CHOPPED
PEPPER
4 PORK STEAKS,
TRIMMED OF ALL VISIBLE FAT
OLIVE OIL, FOR BRUSHING

GREMOLATA

3 TBSP FINELY CHOPPED
FRESH PARSLEY
GRATED RIND OF 1 LIME
GRATED RIND OF ½ LEMON
1 GARLIC CLOVE,
VERY FINELY CHOPPED

SERVES 4

Mix the orange juice, vinegar, and garlic together in a shallow, nonmetallic dish and season to taste with pepper. Add the pork, turning to coat. Cover and let marinate in the refrigerator for up to 3 hours.

Meanwhile, mix all the Gremolata ingredients together in a small mixing bowl, then cover with plastic wrap and let chill in the refrigerator until required.

Heat a nonstick ridged skillet pan and brush lightly with olive oil. Remove the pork from the marinade, reserving the marinade, and add to the pan. Cook over medium–high heat for 5 minutes on each side, or until the juices run clear when the meat is pierced with the tip of a sharp knife.

Meanwhile, pour the marinade into a small pan and let simmer over medium heat for 5 minutes, or until slightly thickened. Transfer the pork to a serving dish, then pour the orange sauce over it and sprinkle with the Gremolata. Serve immediately.

PORK WITH FENNEL
AND JUNIPER

½ FENNEL BULB

1 TBSP JUNIPER BERRIES

ABOUT 2 TBSP OLIVE OIL

FINELY GRATED RIND AND
JUICE OF 1 ORANGE

4 PORK CHOPS,
EACH ABOUT 5½ OZ/150 G

TO SERVE
FRESH BREAD AND
A CRISP SALAD

VARIATION
FOR A VARIATION ON THIS
JUNIPER SAUCE,
SEE PAGE 10

SERVES 4

Finely chop the fennel bulb, discarding the green parts.

Grind the juniper berries in a pestle and mortar. Mix the crushed juniper berries with the fennel flesh, olive oil and orange rind.

Using a sharp knife, score a few cuts all over each chop.

Place the pork chops in a roasting pan or an ovenproof dish. Spoon the fennel and juniper mixture over the chops.

Pour the orange juice over the top of each chop, cover and marinate in the refrigerator for about 2 hours.

Cook the pork chops, under a preheated broiler, for 10–15 minutes, depending on the thickness of the meat, or until the meat is tender and cooked through, turning occasionally.

Transfer the pork chops to serving plates and serve with a crisp, fresh salad and plenty of fresh bread to mop up the cooking juices.

HONEY-GLAZED PORK CHOPS

4 LEAN PORK LOIN CHOPS

SALT AND PEPPER

4 TBSP CLEAR HONEY

1 TBSP DRY SHERRY

4 TBSP ORANGE JUICE

2 TBSP OLIVE OIL

1-INCH/2.5-CM PIECE FRESH
GINGERROOT, GRATED

CORN OIL, FOR OILING

SERVES 4

Preheat the barbecue. Season the pork chops with salt and
pepper to taste. Reserve while you make the glaze.

To make the glaze, place the honey, sherry, orange juice,
olive oil, and gingerroot in a small pan and heat gently,
stirring constantly, until well blended.

Cook the pork chops on an oiled rack over hot coals for
5 minutes on each side.

Brush the chops with the glaze and cook for an additional
2–4 minutes on each side, basting frequently with the glaze.

Transfer the pork chops to warmed serving plates and serve hot.

Alternative Cooking Method

A grill pan or skillet can also be used to cook these pork chops.
Ensure that you brush the pan with a little oil first and then
pre-heat before adding the meat. Cooking times may be increased
slightly as this method of cooking does not generate the high
heat of a barbecue. You therefore will need to look for visual signs
that the food is cooked to your liking.

LAMB CHOPS WITH ROSEMARY

8 LAMB CHOPS

5 TBSP OLIVE OIL

2 TBSP LEMON JUICE

1 GARLIC CLOVE, CRUSHED

½ TSP LEMON PEPPER

SALT

8 FRESH ROSEMARY SPRIGS

SALAD

4 TOMATOES, SLICED

4 SCALLIONS, DIAGONALLY SLICED

DRESSING

2 TBSP OLIVE OIL

1 TBSP LEMON JUICE

1 GARLIC CLOVE, CHOPPED

¼ TSP FINELY CHOPPED FRESH
ROSEMARY

SERVES 4

Preheat the barbecue. Trim the lamb by cutting away the flesh to expose the tips of the bones.

Place the oil, lemon juice, garlic, lemon pepper, and salt in a shallow nonmetallic dish and whisk with a fork to combine.

Lay the rosemary in the dish and place the lamb on top. Cover and let marinate in the refrigerator for at least 1 hour, turning once.

Remove the chops from the marinade and wrap foil around the exposed bones to stop them from burning.

Place the rosemary sprigs on the rack and place the lamb on top. Cook over hot coals for 10–15 minutes, turning once.

Meanwhile, make the salad and dressing. Arrange the tomatoes on a serving dish and sprinkle the scallions on top. Place all the ingredients for the dressing in a screw-top jar, then shake well and pour over the salad. Serve with the lamb chops.

Alternative Cooking Method
A grill pan or skillet can also be used to cook these lamb cutlets. Ensure that you brush the pan with a little oil first and then pre-heat before adding the meat. Cooking times may be increased slightly as this method of cooking does not generate the high heat of a barbecue. You therefore will need to look for visual signs that the food is cooked to your liking.

PORK IN LEMON SAUCE

4 PORK CHOPS (OR LOIN STEAKS)
PEPPER
2 TBSP OLIVE OIL
BUNCH SCALLIONS,
WHITE PARTS ONLY, SLICED THINLY
1 ROMAINE LETTUCE,
SLICED THINLY WIDTHWISE
1 TBSP CHOPPED FRESH DILL
1 CUP CHICKEN STOCK
2 EGGS
JUICE OF 1 LARGE LEMON
SALT

SERVES 4

Season the pork chops with pepper. Heat the oil in a large, heavy-bottomed skillet, add the scallions and fry for 2 minutes until softened. Add the pork chops and fry for 10 minutes, turning the chops several times, until browned on both sides and tender.

When the pork chops are cooked, add the lettuce, dill, and stock to the skillet. Bring to the boil, cover, and then simmer for 4–5 minutes, until the lettuce has wilted.

Meanwhile, put the eggs and lemon juice in a large bowl and whisk together.

When the lettuce has wilted remove the pork chops and lettuce from the skillet with a slotted spoon, put in a warmed serving dish and keep warm in a low oven. Strain the cooking liquid into a measuring jug.

Gradually add 4 tablespoons of the hot cooking liquid to the lemon mixture, whisking all the time. Pour the egg mixture into the skillet and simmer for 2–3 minutes, whisking all the time, until the sauce thickens. (Do not boil or the sauce will curdle.) Season with salt and pepper. Pour the sauce over the pork chops and lettuce and serve hot.

PORK CHOPS AND
SPICY BEANS

3 TBSP VEGETABLE OIL

4 LEAN PORK CHOPS,
RIND REMOVED

2 ONIONS, PEELED AND
THINLY SLICED

2 GARLIC CLOVES,
PEELED AND CRUSHED

2 FRESH GREEN CHILIES,
SEEDED AND CHOPPED OR USE
1-2 TSP MINCED CHILI

1 INCH/2.5 CM PIECE GINGERROOT,
PEELED AND CHOPPED

1½ TSP CUMIN SEEDS

1½ TSP GROUND CORIANDER

2 CUPS STOCK OR WATER

2 TBSP TOMATO PASTE

½ EGGPLANT, TRIMMED AND
CUT INTO ½ INCH/1 CM DICE

SALT

14 OZ/1 X 400 G CAN RED KIDNEY
BEANS, DRAINED

4 TBSP HEAVY CREAM

TO GARNISH

SPRIGS OF CILANTRO

SERVES 4

Heat the vegetable oil in a large frying skillet, add the pork chops and fry until sealed and browned on both sides. Remove from the pan and set aside until required.

Add the sliced onions, garlic, chillies, ginger and spices and fry gently for 2 minutes. Stir in the stock or water, tomato paste, diced eggplant and season with salt and pepper.

Bring the mixture to the boil, place the pork chops on top, then cover and simmer gently over medium heat for 30 minutes.

Remove the chops for a moment and stir the red kidney beans and heavy cream into the mixture. Return the chops to the pan, cover and heat through gently for 5 minutes.

Taste and adjust the seasoning, if necessary. Serve hot, garnished with cilantro sprigs.

VEAL CHOPS WITH WILD MUSHROOM SAUCE

4 VEAL LOIN CHOPS,
¾ INCH/2 CM THICK

GARLIC- OR PAPRIKA-FLAVORED
OLIVE OIL

SALT AND PEPPER

FOR THE WILD MUSHROOM SAUCE

1¼ CUPS MADEIRA

½ STICK BUTTER

2 SHALLOTS, FINELY CHOPPED

1 LB 2 OZ/500 G MIXED WILD
MUSHROOMS, SUCH AS CÈPES,
CHANTERELLES, MORELS, AND
SHIITAKES, WIPED AND TRIMMED,
AND SLICED IF LARGE

GENEROUS 2 CUPS VEGETABLE
STOCK

FRESHLY GRATED NUTMEG

SALT AND PEPPER

SERVES 4

To make the Wild Mushroom Sauce, put the Madeira in a small pan over high heat and boil until it reduces by half, then set aside. Melt the butter in a large sauté pan or skillet over medium-high heat. Add the shallots and sauté for 2–3 minutes, or until soft, but not brown.

Stir the mushrooms into the pan and continue sautéeing until they give off their liquid. Pour in the stock and bring to a boil, stirring. Reduce the heat to low and let the stock simmer until it reduces by half. Stir in the reduced Madeira and continue simmering until only about 6 tablespoons of the liquid are left. Add a few gratings of nutmeg, then season to taste with salt and pepper.

Meanwhile, preheat the broiler to high. Brush the veal chops with oil and season to taste with salt and pepper. Transfer to the broiler rack. Broil the veal chops for 3 minutes. Turn them over, then brush again with the oil and season to taste with salt and pepper. Continue broiling for an additional 3–4 minutes, or until tender and cooked. Transfer the chops to serving plates and spoon the Wild Mushroom Sauce alongside.

VEAL CHOPS WITH SALSA VERDE

4 VEAL CHOPS, SUCH AS LOIN
CHOPS, ABOUT 8 OZ
EACH AND ¾ INCH THICK
GARLIC-FLAVORED OLIVE OIL,
FOR BRUSHING
SALT AND PEPPER

SALSA VERDE
2 OZ FRESH FLAT-LEAF
PARSLEY LEAVES
3 CANNED ANCHOVY FILLETS IN
OIL, DRAINED
½ TBSP CAPERS IN BRINE,
RINSED AND DRAINED
1 SHALLOT, FINELY CHOPPED
1 GARLIC CLOVE, HALVED, GREEN
CORE REMOVED AND CHOPPED
1 TBSP LEMON JUICE, OR TO TASTE
6 LARGE FRESH BASIL LEAVES
2 SPRIGS FRESH OREGANO
½ CUP EXTRA-VIRGIN OLIVE OIL

TO GARNISH
FRESH BASIL OR
OREGANO LEAVES

SERVES 4

To make the salsa verde, put all the ingredients, except the olive oil, in a blender or food processor and process until they are chopped and blended.

With the motor running, add the oil through the top or feed tube and quickly blend until thickened. Add pepper to taste. Transfer to a bowl, cover, and chill.

Lightly brush the veal chops with olive oil and season them with salt and pepper. Place under a preheated broiler and cook for about 3 minutes. Turn over, brush with more oil, and broil for a further 2 minutes until cooked when tested with the tip of a knife.

Transfer the chops to individual plates and spoon a little of the chilled salsa verde beside them. Garnish the chops with fresh oregano or basil and serve with the remaining salsa verde, passed separately.

3 ROASTS

Roasts are much easier to cook than many people think and are ideal for family gatherings and entertaining guests. They look impressive, smell appetizing, taste wonderful, and the choice of different meats, particular cuts, and methods of preparation is huge. Whether your taste is for the traditional, such as Roast Pork with Crackling (see page 134), the sophisticated, such as Festive Beef Wellington (see page 160), the exotic, such as Red Roast Pork in Soy Sauce (see page 146), or the unusual, such as Slow-cooked Lamb with Orzo (see page 148), you are sure to find the perfect recipe for any occasion.

ROAST LOIN OF
PORK

2 LB 4 OZ/1 KG PIECE OF PORK LOIN,
CHINED (BACKBONE REMOVED)
AND THE RIND SCORED BY
THE BUTCHER

1 TBSP ALL-PURPOSE FLOUR

1¼ CUPS HARD CIDER,
APPLE JUICE, CHICKEN STOCK, OR
VEGETABLE STOCK

STUFFING

1 TBSP MELTED BUTTER

½ ONION, PEELED AND
FINELY CHOPPED

1 GARLIC CLOVE, PEELED AND
FINELY CHOPPED

½ INCH/1 CM PIECE FRESH
GINGERROOT, PEELED AND
FINELY CHOPPED

1 PEAR, CORED AND CHOPPED

6 FRESH SAGE LEAVES, CHOPPED

1 CUP FRESH BREAD CRUMBS,
WHITE OR WHOLE-WHEAT

SALT AND PEPPER

TO SERVE

ROAST POTATOES AND
COOKED SEASONAL VEGETABLES

SERVES 4

Preheat the oven to 425°F/220°C. Make the stuffing by heating the butter in a small pan and cooking the onion and garlic over medium heat for 3 minutes until soft. Add the ginger and pear, mix well, and cook for 1 minute more.

Remove from the heat and stir in the sage and bread crumbs, and season well.

Put the stuffing along the middle of the loin, then roll it up, and tie with string; you will need 4–5 pieces to hold the roast in shape. You can cover the stuffing on the ends with small pieces of foil to stop it burning.

Season well, and in particular use a lot of salt on the rind to make crisp crackling. Place the meat in a roasting pan and roast in the center of the preheated oven for 20 minutes.

Reduce the oven temperature to 350°F/180°C and cook for an hour until the skin is crispy and the juices run clear when the joint is pierced with a skewer.

Remove from the oven, lift out the meat, and place on a hot serving plate. Cover with foil and leave in a warm place.

Pour off most of the fat from the roasting pan, leaving the meat juices and sediments behind. Sprinkle in the flour and whisk well. Cook the paste for a couple of minutes, then add the cider, apple juice, or stock, a little at a time, until you have a smooth gravy. Boil for 2–3 minutes until the gravy is the required consistency. Season well and pour into a hot serving pitcher.

Cut the string from the roast and remove the crackling by cutting into the fat. Carve the stuffed pork into slices and serve on hot plates with the crackling and the gravy. Serve with roast potatoes and cooked vegetables in season.

STUFFED SHOULDER
OF LAMB

4 LB/1.8 KG SHOULDER OF
LAMB, BONED
SALT AND PEPPER

SERVES 6-8

STUFFING

1 TBSP BUTTER, MELTED
1 ONION, PEELED AND
FINELY CHOPPED
1 GARLIC CLOVE, PEELED AND
FINELY CHOPPED
4 OZ/115 G GROUND VEAL OR PORK
2 CUPS FRESH BREAD CRUMBS,
WHITE OR WHOLE-WHEAT
GRATED RIND AND JUICE OF
1 LEMON
1 TBSP CHOPPED FRESH PARSLEY
1 TBSP CHOPPED FRESH ROSEMARY
1 TBSP OLIVE OIL
1 CUP RED WINE

TO SERVE

SMALL NAVY BEANS, COOKED WITH
A CRUSHED CLOVE OF GARLIC AND
1 TBSP CHOPPED FRESH PARSLEY

Preheat the oven to 400ºF/200°C. Wipe the lamb with paper towels and season well inside and out. To make the stuffing, melt the butter in a small pan and cook the onion and garlic over medium heat for about 3 minutes until soft and transparent. Transfer to a large bowl and combine with the veal, bread crumbs, lemon rind and juice, and herbs.

Season the mixture well. Using your hands, carefully put the stuffing into the shoulder.

Sew up the pocket to form a good shape (do not worry about the stitches – they will be removed – but try to use only one piece of string).

Place the lamb in a roasting pan and rub it with the oil. Season with salt and pepper and roast in the center of the preheated oven for 1½ hours, basting from time to time.

Remove the pan from the oven, then lift out the meat, and place on a warm serving plate. Remove all the string, cover the meat with foil, and keep it warm.

Pour off the excess fat from the pan and make gravy with the juices. Add the red wine, scrape all the sediment off the base of the pan, and boil vigorously for 2–3 minutes until well reduced. Pour the gravy into a warm pitcher. Serve the lamb thickly sliced with small navy beans, simply heated with a crushed clove of garlic and a tablespoon of chopped parsley.

SLOW-ROASTED PORK

3 LB 8 OZ/1.6 KG LOIN OF PORK,
BONED AND ROLLED
4 GARLIC CLOVES,
SLICED THINLY LENGTHWISE
1½ TSP FINELY CHOPPED FRESH
FENNEL FRONDS OR
½ TSP DRIED FENNEL
4 CLOVES
SALT AND PEPPER
1¼ CUPS DRY WHITE WINE
1¼ CUPS WATER

SERVES 6

Use a small, sharp knife to make incisions all over the pork, opening them out slightly to make little pockets. Place the garlic slices in a small strainer and rinse under cold running water to moisten. Spread out the fennel on a saucer and roll the garlic slices in it to coat. Slide the garlic slices and the cloves into the pockets in the pork. Season the meat all over with salt and pepper.

Place the pork in a large ovenproof dish or roasting pan. Pour in the wine and water. Cook in a preheated oven, 300°F/150ºC, basting the meat occasionally, for 2½–2¾ hours, until the pork is tender but still quite moist.

If you are serving the pork hot, transfer it to a carving board and cut into slices. If you are serving it cold, let it cool completely in the cooking juices before removing and slicing.

STUFFED PORK FILLET

2 PORK FILLETS,
ABOUT 1 LB 2 OZ/500 G EACH,
TRIMMED OF ALL VISIBLE FAT

DRESSING

2 RED ONIONS, FINELY CHOPPED

2 CUPS FRESH WHOLE-WHEAT
BREAD CRUMBS

½ CUP NO-SOAK DRIED
PRUNES, CHOPPED

½ CUP NO-SOAK DRIED
APRICOTS, CHOPPED

PINCH OF GRATED NUTMEG

PINCH OF GROUND CINNAMON

SALT AND PEPPER

1 EGG WHITE, LIGHTLY BEATEN

SERVES 8

Preheat the oven to 400°F/200°C. To make the dressing, mix the onions, bread crumbs, prunes, and apricots together. Season to taste with nutmeg, cinnamon, and salt and pepper. Stir in the egg white.

Cut a 5-inch/13-cm long piece from the narrow end of each pork fillet, then cut all the pieces almost completely in half lengthwise and open them out. Spread half the filling evenly over one of the longer pieces, then cover with both the smaller pieces, overlapping the narrow ends slightly. Spread the remaining filling on top and cover with the remaining piece of pork. Tie the pork loaf together with string or trussing thread at intervals along its length. Wrap it securely in foil and place in a roasting pan.

Cook the pork in the preheated oven for 1½ hours. If serving hot, let stand for 10 minutes before unwrapping, cutting off the string, and slicing. If serving cold, let cool in the wrapping, then let chill in the refrigerator for at least 2 hours and up to 6 hours before unwrapping and slicing.

CHA SIU

1 LB 8 OZ/675 G PORK LOIN

3 TBSP HONEY, DISSOLVED IN
1 TBSP BOILING WATER

FOR THE MARINADE
1 TBSP YELLOW BEAN SAUCE,
LIGHTLY CRUSHED
1 TBSP RED FERMENTED BEANCURD
1 TBSP HOISIN SAUCE
1 TBSP OYSTER SAUCE
1 TBSP DARK SOY SAUCE
1 TBSP SUGAR
2 TBSP SHAOXING RICE WINE
1 TSP SESAME OIL

SERVES 4-6

Combine all the marinade ingredients together. Cut the pork loin lengthwise into 2 pieces. Arrange in a single layer in a dish and pour the marinade over the top. Cover and let marinate for at least 2 hours, basting occasionally.

Preheat the oven to 425°F/220°C. On a wire cooling rack, lay out the pieces of pork in a single layer, reserving the marinade. Place the rack over a roasting pan of boiling water and bake for about 15 minutes, insuring that there is always a little water in the pan.

Reduce the oven temperature to 350°F/180°C. Turn the strips over and baste with the marinade. Cook for an additional 10 minutes.

Remove from the oven and preheat the broiler. Brush the pork with the honey and place under the broiler for a few minutes, turning once. Cool and use as required, cut into chunks, thin slices, or tiny cubes.

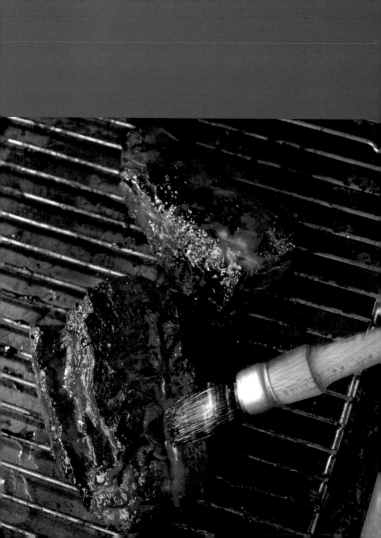

PORK STUFFED WITH
PROSCIUTTO

1 LB 2 OZ/500 G PIECE OF LEAN
PORK FILLET

SMALL BUNCH FRESH OF BASIL
LEAVES, WASHED

2 TBSP FRESHLY GRATED
PARMESAN

2 TBSP SUN-DRIED TOMATO PASTE

6 THIN SLICES PROSCIUTTO

1 TBSP OLIVE OIL

SALT AND PEPPER

OLIVE PASTE

4½ OZ/125 G PITTED BLACK OLIVES

4 TBSP OLIVE OIL

2 GARLIC CLOVES, PEELED

TO SERVE

SALAD LEAVES

SERVES 4

Trim away excess fat and membrane from the pork fillet. Slice the pork lengthways down the middle, taking care not to cut all the way through.

Open out the pork and season the inside. Lay the basil leaves down the centre. Mix the cheese and sun-dried tomato paste and spread over the basil.

Press the pork back together. Wrap the ham around the pork, overlapping, to cover. Place on a rack in a roasting pan, seamside down, and brush with oil. Bake in a preheated oven, 375°F/190°C, for 30–40 minutes depending on thickness until cooked through. Allow to stand for 10 minutes.

For the olive paste, place all the ingredients in a blender or food processor and blend until smooth. Alternatively, for a coarser paste, finely chop the olives and garlic and mix with the oil.

Drain the cooked pork and slice thinly. Serve with the olive paste and a salad.

ROAST PORK WITH
CRACKLING

1 PIECE OF PORK LOIN,
WEIGHING 2 LB 4 OZ/1 KG,
BONED AND THE RIND REMOVED
AND RESERVED

2 TBSP MUSTARD

SALT AND PEPPER

GRAVY

1 TBSP FLOUR

1¼ CUPS CIDER, APPLE JUICE, OR
CHICKEN STOCK

APPLE SAUCE

1 LB/450 G TART COOKING APPLES

3 TBSP WATER

1 TBSP SUPERFINE SUGAR

½ TSP GROUND CINNAMON
(OPTIONAL)

1 TBSP BUTTER (OPTIONAL)

SERVES 4

Preheat the oven to 400°F/200°C.

Score the pork rind thoroughly with a sharp knife and sprinkle with salt. Place it on a wire rack on a baking sheet and roast in the oven for 30–40 minutes until the crackling is golden brown and crisp. This can be cooked in advance, leaving room in the oven for roast potatoes.

Season the pork well with salt and pepper and spread the fat with the mustard. Place in a roasting pan and roast in the center of the oven for 20 minutes. Reduce the oven temperature to 375°F/190°C and cook for an additional 50–60 minutes until the meat is a good color and the juices run clear when it is pierced with a skewer.

Remove the meat from the oven and place on a warmed serving plate, cover with foil, and let stand in a warm place.

To make the gravy, pour off most of the fat from the roasting pan, leaving the meat juices and the sediment. Place the pan over low heat. Sprinkle in the flour, whisking well. Cook the paste for a couple of minutes, then add the cider a little at a time until you have a smooth gravy. Boil for 2–3 minutes until it is the required consistency. Season well with salt and pepper and pour into a warmed serving pitcher.

Carve the pork into slices and serve on warmed plates with pieces of the crackling and the gravy.

To make the Apple Sauce, peel, core, and slice the cooking apples into a medium pan. Add the water and sugar, and cook over low heat for 10 minutes, stirring occasionally. A little ground cinnamon and butter can be added, if you like. Beat well until the sauce is thick and smooth—use a hand mixer for a really smooth finish. Serve the pork with the Apple Sauce.

VITELLO TONNATO

1 BONED AND ROLLED PIECE OF
VEAL LEG, ABOUT 2 LB
BONED WEIGHT
OLIVE OIL
SALT AND PEPPER

TUNA MAYONNAISE
5½ OZ CAN TUNA IN OLIVE OIL
2 LARGE EGGS
ABOUT 3 TBSP LEMON JUICE
OLIVE OIL

8 BLACK OLIVES,
PITTED AND HALVED
1 TBSP CAPERS IN BRINE,
RINSED AND DRAINED
FINELY CHOPPED FRESH
FLAT-LEAF PARSLEY

TO GARNISH
LEMON WEDGES

SERVES 6-8

Rub the veal all over with oil and pepper and place in a roasting pan. Cover the pan with a piece of aluminum foil if there isn't any fat on the meat, then roast in a preheated oven at 450°F/230°C for 10 minutes. Lower the heat to 350°F/175°C and continue roasting for 1 hour for medium, or 1¼ hours if you prefer your veal well done. Set the veal aside and let cool completely, reserving any juices in the roasting pan.

Meanwhile, drain the tuna, reserving the oil. Blend the eggs in a food processor with 1 teaspoon of the lemon juice and a pinch of salt. Add enough olive oil to the tuna oil to make up to 1¼ cups.

With the motor running, add the oil to the eggs, drop by drop, until a thin mayonnaise forms. Add the tuna and process until smooth. Blend in lemon juice to taste. Adjust the seasoning.

Slice the cool meat very thinly. Add any juices to the reserved pan juices. Gradually pour the veal juices into the tuna mayonnaise, whisking until it is a thin, pouring consistency.

Layer the veal slices with the sauce on a platter, ending with a layer of sauce. Cover and chill overnight. Garnish with olives, capers, and a light sprinkling of parsley. Arrange lemon wedges around the edge and serve.

ROAST LAMB WITH GARLIC AND ROSEMARY

1 LEG OF LAMB,
WEIGHING 3 LB 5 OZ/1.5 KG
6 GARLIC CLOVES, THINLY SLICED
LENGTHWISE
8 FRESH ROSEMARY SPRIGS
SALT AND PEPPER
4 TBSP OLIVE OIL

GLAZE
4 TBSP RED CURRANT JELLY
1¼ CUPS BLUSH WINE

SERVES 6

Preheat the oven to 400°F/200°C. Using a small knife, cut slits all over the leg of lamb. Insert 1–2 garlic slices and 4–5 rosemary needles in each slit. Place any remaining rosemary in the bottom of a roasting pan. Season the lamb to taste with salt and pepper and place in the roasting pan. Pour over the oil. Cover with foil and roast for 1 hour 20 minutes.

Mix the red currant jelly and wine together in a small pan. Heat gently, stirring constantly, until combined. Bring to a boil, then reduce the heat and let simmer until reduced. Remove the lamb from the oven and pour over the glaze. Return to the oven and cook, uncovered, for about 10 minutes, depending on how well done you like it.

Remove the lamb from the roasting pan, tent with foil, and let rest for 15 minutes before carving and serving.

BAKED HAM
WITH SAUCE

4 LB 8 OZ–6 LB 8 OZ/2–3 KG
WHOLE BONELESS CURED HAM
2 BAY LEAVES
1–2 ONIONS, CUT INTO FOURTHS
2 CARROTS, THICKLY SLICED
6 CLOVES

GLAZE
1 TBSP RED CURRANT JELLY
1 TBSP WHOLE-GRAIN MUSTARD

CUMBERLAND SAUCE
1 ORANGE
3 TBSP RED CURRANT JELLY
2 TBSP LEMON OR LIME JUICE
2 TBSP ORANGE JUICE
2–4 TBSP PORT
1 TBSP WHOLE-GRAIN MUSTARD

TO GARNISH
SALAD GREENS
ORANGE SLICES

SERVES 4-6

Place the ham in a large pan. Add the bay leaves, onions, carrots, and cloves and cover with cold water. Bring to a boil over low heat, then cover and simmer for half the cooking time. To calculate the cooking time, allow 30 minutes per 1 lb 2 oz/500 g plus 30 minutes.

Preheat the oven to 350°F/180°C. Drain the meat and remove the skin. Place the meat in a roasting pan and score the fat. To make the glaze, combine the ingredients and spread over the fat. Cook in the oven for the remainder of the cooking time. Baste at least once.

To make the sauce, pare the rind from half the orange and cut into strips. Cook in boiling water for 3 minutes. Drain.

Place all the remaining sauce ingredients in a small pan and heat gently, stirring occasionally, until the red currant jelly dissolves. Add the orange rind strips and simmer gently for an additional 3–4 minutes.

Slice the ham and place on a warmed serving platter. Garnish with salad greens and orange slices and serve with the Cumberland Sauce.

LAMB SHANKS BRAISED WITH GARLIC

1 TSP CORIANDER SEEDS

1 TSP CUMIN SEEDS

1 TSP GROUND CINNAMON

1 FRESH GREEN CHILI, SEEDED
AND FINELY CHOPPED

1 GARLIC BULB, SEPARATED INTO
CLOVES AND PEELED

½ CUP PEANUT OR CORN OIL

GRATED RIND OF 1 LIME

4 LAMB SHANKS

2 ONIONS, CHOPPED

2 CARROTS, CHOPPED

2 CELERY STALKS, CHOPPED

½ SMALL LIME, CHOPPED

ABOUT 3 CUPS BEEF
STOCK OR WATER

1 TSP SUNDRIED TOMATO PASTE

2 FRESH ROSEMARY SPRIGS

SALT AND PEPPER

TO GARNISH

2 FRESH MINT SPRIGS

SERVES 4

Dry-fry the seeds in a skillet until fragrant. Combine the seeds, cinnamon, chili, and 2 garlic cloves in a mortar and pound with a pestle. Stir in half the oil and the lime rind. Rub over the lamb, cover, and let marinate in the refrigerator for 4 hours.

Preheat the oven to 400°F/200°C. Heat the remaining oil in a skillet. Brown the lamb all over and transfer to an ovenproof casserole dish. Chop the remaining garlic. Add to the casserole dish with the onions, carrots, celery, lime, and stock or water to cover. Stir in the tomato paste, herbs, and season to taste with salt and pepper.

Cover and cook in the oven for 30 minutes. Reduce the temperature to 325°F/160°C. Cook for an additional 3 hours, or until very tender.

Transfer the lamb to a dish and keep warm. Strain the cooking juices into a pan. Boil until reduced. Pour over the lamb, garnish with mint, and serve.

POT ROASTED LEG OF LAMB

3½ LB/1.75 KG LEG OF LAMB

3–4 SPRIGS FRESH ROSEMARY

4½ OZ/125 G STREAKY
BACON RASHERS

4 TBSP OLIVE OIL

2–3 GARLIC CLOVES, CRUSHED

2 ONIONS, SLICED

2 CARROTS, SLICED

2 CELERY STALKS, SLICED

1 CUP DRY WHITE WINE

1 TBSP TOMATO PASTE

1 CUP STOCK

12 OZ/350 G TOMATOES, PEELED,
QUARTERED AND DESEEDED

1 TBSP CHOPPED FRESH PARSLEY

1 TBSP CHOPPED FRESH OREGANO
OR MARJORAM

SALT AND PEPPER

TO GARNISH

FRESH ROSEMARY SPRIGS

SERVES 4

Wipe the joint of lamb all over, trimming off any excess fat, then season well with salt and pepper, rubbing well in. Lay the sprigs of rosemary over the lamb, cover evenly with the bacon rashers and tie in place with string.

Heat the oil in a frying skillet and fry the lamb for about 10 minutes or until browned all over, turning several times. Remove from the pan.

Transfer the oil from the frying skillet to a large fireproof casserole dish and fry the garlic and onion together for 3–4 minutes until beginning to soften. Add the carrots and celery and continue to cook for a few minutes longer.

Lay the lamb on top of the vegetables and press down to partly submerge. Pour the wine over the lamb, add the tomato paste and simmer for 3–4 minutes. Add the stock, tomatoes and herbs and seasoning and bring back to the boil for a further 3–4 minutes.

Cover the casserole dish tightly and cook in a moderate oven, 350°F/180°C, for 2–2½ hours until very tender.

Remove the lamb from the casserole dish and if preferred, take off the bacon and herbs along with the string. Keep warm. Strain the juices, skimming off any excess fat, and serve in a jug. The vegetables may be put around the joint or in a serving dish. Garnish with fresh sprigs of rosemary.

ROAST PORK IN SOY SAUCE

1 LB/450 G LEAN PORK FILLETS
6 TBSP DARK SOY SAUCE
2 TBSP DRY SHERRY
1 TSP FIVE-SPICE POWDER
2 GARLIC CLOVES, CRUSHED
1 INCH/2.5 CM PIECE FRESH
GINGERROOT, FINELY CHOPPED
1 LARGE RED BELL PEPPER
1 LARGE YELLOW BELL PEPPER
1 LARGE ORANGE BELL PEPPER
4 TBSP SUPERFINE SUGAR
2 TBSP RED WINE VINEGAR

TO GARNISH
SPRING SCALLIONS, SHREDDED
FRESH CHIVES, SNIPPED

SERVES 4

Trim away any excess fat and silver skin from the pork and place in a shallow dish.

Mix together the soy sauce, sherry, five-spice powder, garlic and ginger. Spoon over the pork, cover and marinate in the refrigerator for at least 1 hour or until required.

Preheat the oven to 375°F/190°C. Drain the pork, reserving the marinade.

Place the pork on a roasting rack over a roasting pan. Cook in the oven, occasionally basting with the marinade, for 1 hour or until cooked through.

Meanwhile, halve and deseed the bell peppers. Cut each bell pepper half into 3 equal portions. Arrange them on a cookie sheet and bake alongside the pork for the last 30 minutes of cooking time.

Place the superfine sugar and vinegar in a saucepan and heat gently until the sugar dissolves. Bring to the boil and simmer for 3–4 minutes, until syrupy.

When the pork is cooked, remove it from the oven and brush with the sugar syrup. Leave for about 5 minutes, then slice and arrange on a serving platter with the bell peppers, garnished with the spring scallions and chives.

Serve garnished with the spring scallions and freshly snipped chives.

SLOW-COOKED LAMB
WITH ORZO

2 LARGE GARLIC CLOVES
1 UNBONED SHOULDER OF LAMB
2 X 14 OZ CANS CHOPPED
TOMATOES
4 SPRIGS FRESH THYME
4 SPRIGS FRESH PARSLEY
1 BAY LEAF
½ CUP WATER
9 OZ ORZO PASTA
SALT AND PEPPER

TO SERVE
FRESH THYME SPRIGS

SERVES 6

Cut the garlic cloves in half and remove the green cores, then thinly slice. Using the tip of a sharp knife, make slits all over the lamb shoulder, then insert the garlic slices into the slits.

Pour the tomatoes and their juices into a roasting pan large enough to hold the lamb shoulder. Add the thyme, parsley, and bay leaf. Place the lamb on top, skin-side up, and cover the dish tightly with a sheet of foil, shiny side down. Scrunch the foil all around the edge so that none of the juices escape during cooking.

Put in a preheated oven at 325°F/160°C and cook for 3½–4 hours until the lamb is tender and the tomatoes are reduced to a thick sauce.

Remove the lamb from the roasting pan and set aside. Using a large metal spoon, skim off as much fat from the surface of the tomato sauce as possible.

Add the water and orzo to the tomatoes, stirring so the grains are submerged. Add a little extra water if the sauce seems too thick. Season to taste with salt and pepper. Return the lamb to the roasting pan.

Re-cover the roasting pan and return to the oven for 15 minutes, or until the orzo is tender. Remove the bay leaf. Let the lamb rest for 10 minutes, then slice and serve with the orzo in tomato juice, garnished with fresh thyme sprigs.

ROASTED RED PORK

1 LB 5 OZ/600 G PORK TENDERLOIN

MARINADE

2 GARLIC CLOVES, CRUSHED

1 TBSP GRATED FRESH
GINGERROOT, GRATED

1 TBSP LIGHT SOY SAUCE

1 TBSP THAI FISH SAUCE

1 TBSP RICE WINE

1 TBSP HOISIN SAUCE

1 TBSP SESAME OIL

1 TBSP PALM SUGAR OR
BROWN SUGAR

½ TSP CHINESE FIVE-SPICE POWDER

A FEW DROPS RED FOOD
COLORING

TO GARNISH

RED CHILI FLOWER

TO SERVE

NAPA CABBAGE, SHREDDED

SERVES 4

Combine all the ingredients for the marinade and spread the mixture over the pork, turning to coat evenly. Place in a large dish, cover, and set aside in the refrigerator to marinate overnight.

Place a rack in a roasting pan, then half-fill the pan with boiling water. Lift the pork from the marinade and place on the rack. Reserve the marinade for later.

Roast in a preheated oven, 425°F/220°C, for about 20 minutes. Baste with the reserved marinade, then lower the heat to 350°F/180°C and continue roasting for a further 35–40 minutes, basting occasionally with the marinade, until the pork is a rich reddish brown and thoroughly cooked.

Transfer the pork to a cutting board and cut into even slices. Arrange the slices on a bed of shredded Napa cabbage on a serving platter, garnish with a red chili flower, and serve immediately.

SAUERBRATEN

1 LB 10 OZ/750 G TOP ROUND OF
BEEF, TRIMMED OF ALL VISIBLE FAT

8 WHOLE CLOVES

1 TBSP CORN OIL

1 CUP BEEF STOCK

2 LB 4 OZ/1 KG MIXED ROOT
VEGETABLES, SUCH AS CARROTS,
POTATOES, AND RUTABAGA,
PEELED AND CUT INTO CHUNKS

2 TBSP RAISINS

1½ TSP CORNSTARCH

3 TBSP WATER

SALT AND PEPPER

MARINADE

¾ CUP WINE

5 TBSP RED WINE VINEGAR

1 ONION, CHOPPED

1½ TSP BROWN SUGAR

4 PEPPERCORNS

1 BAY LEAF

½ TSP GROUND ALLSPICE

½ TSP MUSTARD

SERVES 4

To make the marinade, put all the ingredients, except the
mustard, in a pan. Bring to simmering point, then remove from
the heat and stir in the mustard. Stud the beef with cloves and
place in a nonmetallic dish. Pour the marinade over, cover, and
let cool, then let chill in the refrigerator for 2 days. About 1 hour
before cooking, remove the beef, pat dry, and let stand at room
temperature. Set aside the marinade.

Preheat the oven to 300°F/150°C. Heat the oil in an ovenproof
casserole dish, add the beef, and cook over medium heat for
5–10 minutes, or until browned. Pour the marinade into the
casserole dish through a strainer, add the stock, and bring to a
boil. Cover and bake in the oven for 1 hour, turning and basting
frequently with the cooking juices.

Meanwhile, blanch the vegetables in boiling water for 3 minutes,
then drain. Arrange the vegetables round the beef, return to the
oven, and cook for 1 hour, or until the beef is very tender and the
vegetables are cooked.

Transfer the beef and vegetables to a serving dish. Place the
casserole dish on low heat and add the raisins. Mix the cornstarch
and water until smooth and stir into the cooking juices. Bring to
a boil, stirring, then let simmer for 2–3 minutes. Season and serve.

ROAST HAM

1 BONELESS HAM JOINT,
WEIGHING 3 LB/1.3 KG
2 TBSP DIJON MUSTARD
GENEROUS ¾ CUP RAW SUGAR
½ TSP GROUND CINNAMON
½ TSP GROUND GINGER
18 WHOLE CLOVES

CUMBERLAND SAUCE

2 SEVILLE ORANGES, HALVED
4 TBSP RED CURRANT JELLY
4 TBSP PORT
1 TSP MUSTARD
SALT AND PEPPER

SERVES 6

Place the joint in a large pan, cover with cold water, and gradually bring to a boil over low heat. Cover and let simmer very gently for 1 hour.

Preheat the oven to 400°F/200°C.

Remove the ham from the pan and drain. Remove the rind from the ham and discard. Score the fat into a diamond-shaped pattern with a sharp knife. Spread the mustard over the fat. Mix the sugar and ground spices together on a plate and roll the ham in it, pressing down to coat evenly.

Stud the diamond shapes with cloves and place the joint in a roasting pan. Roast in the oven for 20 minutes until the glaze is a rich golden color.

To serve hot, cover with foil and let stand for 20 minutes before carving. If the ham is to be served cold, it can be cooked a day ahead.

To make a Cumberland Sauce, remove the zest of the oranges using a citrus zester. Place the red currant jelly, port, and mustard in a small pan and heat gently until the jelly has melted. Squeeze the juice from the oranges into the pan. Add the orange zest and season to taste with salt and pepper. Serve cold with ham. The sauce can be kept in a screw-top jar in the refrigerator for up to 2 weeks.

ROAST LAMB WITH ROSEMARY
AND MARSALA

4 LB LEG OF LAMB
2 GARLIC CLOVES, SLICED THINLY
2 TBSP ROSEMARY LEAVES
8 TBSP OLIVE OIL
SALT AND PEPPER
2 LB POTATOES,
CUT INTO 1-INCH CUBES
6 FRESH SAGE LEAVES, CHOPPED
⅔ CUP MARSALA

SERVES 6

Use a small, sharp knife to make incisions all over the lamb, opening them out slightly to make little pockets. Insert the garlic slices and about half the rosemary leaves in the pockets.

Place the lamb in a roasting pan and spoon half the olive oil over it. Roast in a preheated oven, 425°F/220°C, for 15 minutes.

Reduce the oven temperature to 350°F/175°C. Remove the lamb from the oven and season to taste with salt and pepper. Turn the lamb over, return to the oven, and roast for an additional hour.

Meanwhile, spread out the cubed potatoes in a second roasting pan, pour the remaining olive oil over them, and toss to coat. Sprinkle with the remaining rosemary and the sage. Place the potatoes in the oven with the lamb and roast for 40 minutes.

Remove the lamb from the oven, turn it over, and pour over the Marsala. Return it to the oven with the potatoes and cook for an additional 15 minutes.

Transfer the lamb to a carving board and cover with foil. Place the roasting pan over high heat and bring the juices to a boil. Continue to boil until thickened and syrupy. Strain into a warmed gravy boat or pitcher.

Carve the lamb into slices and serve with the potatoes and sauce.

STUFFED ROAST PORK
WITH GARLIC

2 LB 4 OZ/1 KG PORK LOIN,
BACKBONE REMOVED AND
RIND SCORED
2 TBSP HONEY

STUFFING
6 TBSP BUTTER
1 GARLIC CLOVE, CHOPPED
2 SHALLOTS, CHOPPED
¾ CUP CHOPPED MUSHROOMS
4 SLICES LEAN BACK BACON,
CHOPPED
1¾ CUPS FRESH BREAD CRUMBS
1 TBSP FINELY CHOPPED
FRESH SAGE
1 TBSP LEMON JUICE
1 TBSP GRATED LEMON RIND
SALT AND PEPPER

TO GARNISH
SPRIGS OF FRESH SAGE

TO SERVE
ROAST POTATOES

SERVES 4

Preheat the oven to 450°F/230°C. To make the stuffing, melt the
butter in a pan over medium heat. Add the garlic and shallots
and cook, stirring, for 3 minutes, or until softened. Add the
mushrooms and bacon, and cook for another 2 minutes. Remove
from the heat and stir in the bread crumbs, sage, lemon juice and
rind, and salt and pepper to taste.

Put the stuffing in the middle of the pork loin, then roll up and
secure the loin with several lengths of tied string. Place the joint
in a roasting pan, then rub the skin with plenty of salt and season
with pepper. Brush the honey over the pork.

Cook in the preheated oven for 25 minutes, then reduce the heat
to 350°F/180°C. Cook, basting occasionally, for about 1¼ hours,
or until cooked through. Remove from the oven and let rest for
15 minutes. Garnish with sage sprigs and serve with roast potatoes.

FESTIVE BEEF
WELLINGTON

1 LB 10 OZ/750 G THICK BEEF FILLET

2 TBSP BUTTER

SALT AND PEPPER

2 TBSP VEGETABLE OIL

1 GARLIC CLOVE, CHOPPED

1 ONION, CHOPPED

6 OZ/175 G CRIMINI MUSHROOMS

1 TBSP CHOPPED FRESH SAGE

SALT AND PEPPER

12 OZ/350 G FROZEN PUFF PASTRY
DOUGH, THAWED

1 EGG, BEATEN

TO GARNISH

CHOPPED FRESH SAGE

SERVES 4

Preheat the oven to 425°F/220°C. Put the beef in a roasting pan, spread with butter, and season. Roast for 30 minutes, then remove from the oven. Meanwhile, heat the oil in a pan over medium heat. Add the garlic and onion and cook, stirring, for 3 minutes. Stir in the mushrooms, sage, and seasoning, and cook for 5 minutes. Remove from the heat.

Roll out the dough into a rectangle large enough to enclose the beef, then place the beef in the middle and spread the mushroom mixture over it. Bring the long sides of the dough together over the beef and seal with beaten egg. Tuck the short ends over (trim away excess dough) and seal. Place on a cookie sheet, seam-side down. Make 2 slits in the top. Decorate with dough shapes and brush with beaten egg. Bake for 40 minutes. If it browns too quickly, cover with foil. Remove from the oven, garnish with sage.

MAPLE ROAST LAMB
WITH CIDER

2 TBSP LEMON-FLAVORED OIL OR
EXTRA-VIRGIN OLIVE OIL
5 LB/2.25 KG LEG OF LAMB
1 GARLIC CLOVE, CHOPPED
1 TBSP CHOPPED FRESH OREGANO
JUICE OF 1 LEMON
3 TBSP MAPLE SYRUP
SALT AND PEPPER
3 CUPS HARD CIDER
1 TBSP CORNSTARCH
2 TBSP WATER

TO GARNISH
SPRIGS OF FRESH OREGANO

TO SERVE
ROAST POTATOES

SERVES 4

Preheat the oven to 400°F/200°C. Pour the oil into a roasting pan. Using a sharp knife, trim off and discard any excess fat from the lamb, then make small incisions all over. Transfer the joint to the roasting pan. Put the garlic into a bowl and add the chopped oregano, lemon juice, maple syrup, and salt and pepper to taste. Mix together well. Pour the mixture evenly over the lamb, pushing it into the incisions, then pour over the cider.

Transfer the pan to the preheated oven and roast for 30 minutes, turning once and basting occasionally. Reduce the oven temperature to 300°F/150°C and cook for a further 2¾ hours, or until tender and cooked through. Lift out and place on a serving platter to rest for 10 minutes. Blend the cornstarch with the water, then stir into the juices in the pan. Transfer to the stove. Stir over low heat until thickened. Garnish the lamb with oregano sprigs. Serve with roast potatoes and the thickened juices.

LAMB SHANKS WITH ROASTED ONIONS

4 12-OZ LAMB SHANKS

6 GARLIC CLOVES

2 TBSP VIRGIN OLIVE OIL

1 TBSP VERY FINELY CHOPPED
FRESH ROSEMARY

PEPPER

4 RED ONIONS

SALT

12 OZ CARROTS,
CUT INTO THIN STICKS

4 TBSP WATER

SERVES 4

Trim off any excess fat from the lamb. Using a small, sharp knife, make 6 incisions in each shank. Cut the garlic cloves lengthwise into 4 slices. Insert 6 garlic slices in the incisions in each lamb shank.

Place the lamb in a single layer in a roasting pan, drizzle with the olive oil, sprinkle with the rosemary, and season with pepper. Roast in a preheated oven, 350°F/175°C, for 45 minutes.

Wrap each of the onions in a square of foil. Remove the roasting pan from the oven and season the lamb shanks with salt. Return the pan to the oven and place the onions on the shelf next to it. Roast for an additional 1-1¼ hours, until the lamb is very tender.

Meanwhile, bring a large pan of water to a boil. Add the carrot sticks and blanch for 1 minute. Drain and refresh under cold water.

Remove the roasting pan from the oven when the lamb is meltingly tender and transfer it to a warmed serving dish. Skim off any fat from the roasting pan and place it over medium heat. Add the carrots and cook for 2 minutes, then add the water, bring to a boil, and let simmer, stirring constantly and scraping up the glazed bits from the bottom of the roasting pan.

Transfer the carrots and sauce to the serving dish. Remove the onions from the oven and unwrap. Cut off and discard about ½ inch of the tops and add the onions to the dish. Serve immediately.

MARINATED ROAST LAMB

SCANT 2 CUPS PLAIN YOGURT

½ CUP LEMON JUICE

3 TBSP MALT VINEGAR

2 TSP CHILI POWDER

2 TSP GINGER PASTE

2 TSP GARLIC PASTE

1 TSP BROWN SUGAR

1 TSP SALT

FEW DROPS RED FOOD COLORING

5 LB 8 OZ/2.5 KG LEG OF LAMB

VEGETABLE OIL, FOR BRUSHING

TO GARNISH

FRESH CILANTRO SPRIGS

SERVES 6

Mix the yogurt, lemon juice, vinegar, chili powder, ginger paste, garlic paste, sugar, salt, and food coloring together in a bowl. Make several deep slashes all over the lamb and place in a large, roasting pan. Pour over the yogurt mixture, turning to coat and pressing it well into the slashes. Cover with plastic wrap and let marinate in the refrigerator for 8 hours or overnight.

Preheat the oven to 375°F/190°C. Remove the lamb from the refrigerator and bring to room temperature. Roast the lamb in the preheated oven for 1¼ hours, basting occasionally with the marinade.

Remove the lamb from the oven and reduce the oven temperature to 325°F/160°C. Place the lamb on a large sheet of foil, brush with vegetable oil, then wrap the foil round the meat to enclose it completely. Return to the oven and roast for an additional 45–60 minutes, or until tender.

Let the lamb rest for 10 minutes before carving and serving, garnished with fresh cilantro sprigs.

ROAST LAMB WITH
BEANS

1⅓ CUPS DRIED
FLAGEOLET BEANS
1 LARGE ONION,
CUT INTO FOURTHS
6 LARGE GARLIC CLOVES
1 BAY LEAF
SPRIGS OF FRESH ROSEMARY
2 LB/900 G BONELESS LEG OF
LAMB, ROLLED AND TIED
2 TSP OLIVE OIL
⅜ STICK UNSALTED BUTTER
2 TBSP CHOPPED FRESH
FLAT-LEAF PARSLEY
⅔ CUP MEDIUM-DRY CIDER
ABOUT ⅔ CUP LAMB STOCK OR
VEGETABLE STOCK
SALT AND PEPPER

SERVES 4-6

Put the beans in a large bowl. Add enough water to cover by 1 inch/2.5 cm and let soak overnight. The next day, drain and rinse the beans. Place the beans in a large pan and cover with twice their depth of water. Turn the heat to high, then bring the water to a boil, skimming the surface as necessary, and boil for 10 minutes.

Drain the beans, then re-cover with more water and return to a boil. Add the onion, 4 of the garlic cloves, and the bay leaf. Reduce the heat to low, then cover the pan and let simmer for 60–90 minutes, or until the beans are tender.

Meanwhile, heat the oven to 350°F/180°C. Cut the remaining 2 cloves of garlic into thin slivers. Insert a couple of rosemary sprigs into the center of the rolled lamb. Use the tip of a knife to make thin cuts all over the lamb, then insert the garlic slivers. Rub the lamb all over with the oil and season to taste with salt and pepper. Scatter over some rosemary leaves.

Place the lamb on a rack in a roasting pan and roast for 1 hour. When the beans are tender, drain them well and discard the onion, garlic, and bay leaf. Stir in the butter, parsley, and salt and pepper to taste. Cover the beans with foil, shiny-side down, and keep warm.

When the lamb is cooked, transfer it to a serving platter, then cover with foil and set aside to rest for 10 minutes. Meanwhile, remove the rack, then tilt the roasting pan and use a large metal spoon to remove the fat from the surface of the pan juices.

Place the pan over medium-high heat and deglaze it by stirring in the cider and scraping the sediment from the bottom of the pan. Bring to a boil and continue boiling until the juices reduce slightly, then add the stock and continue boiling until reduced by half. Season to taste with salt and pepper. Thinly slice the lamb and serve with the beans and pan juices.

ROAST BEEF

1 PRIME RIB OF BEEF JOINT,
WEIGHING 6 LB/2.7 KG

2 TSP DRY ENGLISH MUSTARD

3 TBSP ALL-PURPOSE FLOUR

1¼ CUPS RED WINE

1¼ CUPS BEEF STOCK

2 TSP WORCESTERSHIRE SAUCE
(OPTIONAL)

SALT AND PEPPER

**YORKSHIRE PUDDING
SERVES 4**
PREHEAT THE OVEN TO
425°F/220°C. MAKE A BATTER
WITH 3½ OZ/100 G PLAIN FLOUR,
A PINCH OF SALT, 1 BEATEN EGG
AND 10 FL OZ/300 ML MILK AND
WATER MIXED. ALLOW TO STAND
FOR HALF AN HOUR.
HEAT 2 TBSP ROAST BEEF
DRIPPING OR OLIVE OIL IN
AN 8-INCH SQUARE ROASTING TIN
IN THE TOP OF THE OVEN. REMOVE
THE TIN FROM THE OVEN, POUR IN
THE BATTER AND BAKE FOR 25-30
MINUTES UNTIL IT IS PUFFED UP
AND GOLDEN BROWN.

TO SERVE
YORKSHIRE PUDDING

SERVES 8

Preheat the oven to 450°F/230°C.

Season the meat to taste with salt and pepper. Rub in the mustard and 1 tablespoon of the flour.

Place the meat in a roasting pan large enough to hold it comfortably and roast in the oven for 15 minutes. Reduce the temperature to 375°F/190°C and cook for 15 minutes per 1 lb/450 g, plus 15 minutes (1¾ hours for this joint) for rare beef or 20 minutes per 1 lb/450 g, plus 20 minutes (2 hours 20 minutes) for medium beef. Baste the meat from time to time to keep it moist, and if the pan becomes too dry, add a little stock or red wine.

Remove the meat from the oven and place on a warmed serving plate, cover with foil, and let stand in a warm place for 10–15 minutes.

To make the gravy, pour off most of the fat from the pan (reserve it for cooking the Yorkshire pudding), leaving behind the meat juices and the sediment. Place the pan on the stove over medium heat and scrape all the sediment from the bottom of the pan. Sprinkle in the remaining flour and quickly mix it into the juices with a small whisk. When you have a smooth paste, gradually add the wine and most of the stock, whisking constantly. Bring to a boil, then reduce the heat to a gentle simmer and cook for 2–3 minutes. Season with salt and pepper and add the remaining stock, if needed, and a little Worcestershire sauce, if you like.

When ready to serve, carve the meat into slices and serve on warmed plates. Pour the gravy into a warmed pitcher and take direct to the table. Serve with Yorkshire pudding.

POT-ROAST PORK

1 TBSP CORN OIL
¼ CUP BUTTER
2 LB 4 OZ/1 KG BONED AND
ROLLED PORK LOIN
4 SHALLOTS, CHOPPED
6 JUNIPER BERRIES
2 FRESH THYME SPRIGS, PLUS
EXTRA TO GARNISH
⅔ CUP DRY CIDER
½ CUP CHICKEN STOCK OR WATER
SALT AND PEPPER
8 CELERY STALKS, CHOPPED
2 TBSP ALL-PURPOSE FLOUR
⅔ CUP HEAVY CREAM

TO SERVE

FRESHLY COOKED PEAS

SERVES 4

Heat the oil with half the butter in a heavy-bottomed pan or flameproof casserole dish. Add the pork and cook over medium heat, turning frequently, for 5–10 minutes, or until browned. Transfer to a plate.

Add the shallots to the pan and cook, stirring frequently, for 5 minutes, or until softened. Add the juniper berries and thyme sprigs and return the pork to the pan, with any juices that have collected on the plate. Pour in the cider and stock, season to taste with salt and pepper, then cover and simmer for 30 minutes. Turn the pork over and add the celery. Re-cover the pan and cook for an additional 40 minutes.

Meanwhile, make a beurre manié by mashing the remaining butter with the flour in a small bowl. Transfer the pork and celery to a platter with a perforated spoon and keep warm. Remove and discard the juniper berries and thyme. Whisk the beurre manié, a little at a time, into the simmering cooking liquid. Cook, stirring constantly, for 2 minutes, then stir in the cream and bring to a boil. Slice the pork and spoon a little of the sauce over it. Garnish with thyme sprigs and serve immediately with the celery and freshly cooked peas. Serve the remaining sauce separately.

4 RIBS

Ribs smothered in a sticky sauce, whether cooked on the barbecue, in the oven, or under the broiler, are always fun, not least because you can eat them with your fingers and have the perfect excuse for behaving like a child. They also taste great, whether Hot & Spicy Ribs (see page 176), Chinese Ribs (see page 184), or Spare Ribs with Chili (see page 196). This chapter also includes recipes for those with more adult and sophisticated tastes, such as Crusted Rack of Lamb (see page 178) and Lamb with Balsamic & Rosemary Marinade (see page 200).

HOT AND SPICY RIBS

1 ONION, CHOPPED

2 GARLIC CLOVES, CHOPPED

1-INCH/2.5-CM PIECE FRESH
GINGERROOT, SLICED

1 FRESH RED CHILI, SEEDED
AND CHOPPED

5 TBSP DARK SOY SAUCE

3 TBSP LIME JUICE

1 TBSP JAGGERY OR
BROWN SUGAR

2 TBSP PEANUT OIL

SALT AND PEPPER

2 LB 4 OZ/1 KG PORK SPARERIBS,
SEPARATED

SERVES 4

Preheat the barbecue. Put the onion, garlic, ginger, chili, and soy sauce into a food processor and process to a paste. Transfer to a measuring cup and stir in the lime juice, sugar, and oil. Season with salt and pepper.

Place the spareribs in a preheated wok or large, heavy-bottom pan and pour in the soy sauce mixture. Place on the stove and bring to a boil, then let simmer over low heat, stirring frequently, for 30 minutes. If the mixture appears to be drying out, add a little water.

Remove the spareribs, reserving the sauce. Cook the ribs over medium hot coals, turning and basting frequently with the sauce, for 20–30 minutes. Transfer to a large serving plate and serve immediately.

Alternative Cooking Method

A grill pan or skillet can also be used to cook these ribs. Ensure that you brush the pan with a little oil first and then pre-heat before adding the meat. Cooking times may be increased slightly as this method of cooking does not generate the high heat of a barbecue. You therefore will need to look for visual signs that the food is cooked to your liking.

CRUSTED RACK OF LAMB

2 RACKS OF LAMB,
ABOUT 6–8 CHOPS EACH, SKIN
REMOVED, TRIMMED OF ANY
EXCESS FAT
¼ CUP FRESH WHOLE-WHEAT
BREAD CRUMBS
2–3 GARLIC CLOVES, CRUSHED
2 TBSP CHOPPED FRESH PARSLEY
1 TBSP CHOPPED FRESH MINT
1 TBSP FINELY GRATED
LEMON RIND
SALT AND PEPPER
1 EGG

FOR THE SALSA

1 SMALL GREEN EATING APPLE,
WASHED, CORED, AND FINELY DICED
2 TOMATOES, SEEDED AND
FINELY DICED
3 SCALLIONS, FINELY CHOPPED
1 TBSP CHOPPED FRESH MINT

FOR THE MASH

1 LB/450 G SWEET POTATOES,
PEELED AND CHOPPED
2 TBSP MILK
1 TBSP CHOPPED FRESH MINT

TO SERVE

LIGHTLY COOKED GREEN VEGETABLE,
SUCH AS BROCCOLI

SERVES 4

Preheat the oven to 375°F/190°C. Wipe the lamb racks with paper towels and wrap the ends of the bones with foil.

Mix the bread crumbs, garlic, herbs, lemon rind, and salt and pepper to taste together in a bowl and bind with the egg. Press onto the skinned side of the lamb. Stand the racks in a roasting pan and roast in the preheated oven for 40–50 minutes, or until cooked to your personal preference.

Remove from the oven, remove and discard the foil from the bones, and cover with a sheet of foil. Let rest for 5 minutes.

Meanwhile, mix all the salsa ingredients together in a small serving bowl, cover, and set aside until required.

Cook the sweet potatoes in a pan of lightly salted boiling water for 15–20 minutes, or until tender when pierced with a fork. Drain, mash, then beat in the milk and mint until smooth. Serve the lamb racks with the salsa and mash, accompanied by a lightly cooked green vegetable, such as broccoli.

RACK OF LAMB

1 TRIMMED RACK OF LAMB,
WEIGHING 9–10½ OZ/250–300 G
1 GARLIC CLOVE, CRUSHED
⅔ CUP RED WINE
1 FRESH ROSEMARY SPRIG,
CRUSHED TO RELEASE THE FLAVOR
1 TBSP OLIVE OIL
⅔ CUP LAMB STOCK
2 TBSP RED CURRANT JELLY
SALT AND PEPPER

MINT SAUCE
BUNCH FRESH MINT LEAVES
2 TSP SUPERFINE SUGAR
2 TBSP WATER
2 TBSP WHITE WINE VINEGAR

SERVES 2

Place the rack of lamb in a nonmetallic bowl and rub all over with the garlic. Pour over the wine and place the rosemary sprig on top. Cover and let marinate in the refrigerator for 3 hours or overnight if possible.

Preheat the oven to 425°F/220°C. Remove the lamb from the marinade, reserving the marinade. Pat the meat dry with paper towels and season generously with salt and pepper. Place the lamb in a small roasting pan, drizzle with the oil, and roast for 15–20 minutes, depending on whether you like your meat pink or medium. Remove the lamb from the oven and let rest, covered with foil, in a warm place for 5 minutes.

Meanwhile, pour the reserved marinade into a small pan, bring to a boil over medium heat and bubble gently for 2–3 minutes. Add the stock and red currant jelly and let simmer, stirring, until the mixture is syrupy.

To make the Mint Sauce, chop the fresh mint leaves and mix together with the sugar in a small bowl. Add the boiling water and stir to dissolve the sugar. Add the white wine vinegar and let stand for 30 minutes before serving with the lamb.

Carve the lamb into chops and serve on warmed plates with the sauce spooned over the top. Serve the Mint Sauce separately.

BARBECUE LAMB RIBS

BREAST OF LAMB,
ABOUT 1 LB 9 OZ/700 G

3 TBSP SWEET CHUTNEY

4 TBSP TOMATO KETCHUP

2 TBSP CIDER VINEGAR

2 TSP WORCESTERSHIRE SAUCE

2 TSP MILD MUSTARD

1 TBSP BROWN SUGAR

TO SERVE

SALAD GREENS AND
CHERRY TOMATOES

SERVES 4

Preheat the barbecue. Using a sharp knife, cut between the ribs of the breast of lamb to divide it into slightly smaller pieces.

Bring a large pan of water to a boil. Add the lamb and parboil for 5 minutes. Remove the meat from the water and pat dry thoroughly with paper towels.

Mix the sweet chutney, tomato ketchup, cider vinegar, Worcestershire sauce, mustard, and sugar together in a shallow, nonmetallic dish to make a sauce.

Using a sharp knife, cut the lamb into individual ribs. Add the ribs to the sauce and toss until well coated. Remove the ribs from the sauce, reserving the remaining sauce for basting. Cook the ribs over hot coals for 10–15 minutes, turning and basting frequently with the reserved sauce.

Transfer the ribs to warmed serving plates. Serve immediately with salad greens and cherry tomatoes.

CHINESE
RIBS

2 LB 4 OZ/1 KG PORK SPARERIBS, SEPARATED

4 TBSP DARK SOY SAUCE

3 TBSP BROWN SUGAR

1 TBSP PEANUT OR SUNFLOWER-SEED OIL

2 GARLIC CLOVES, FINELY CHOPPED

2 TSP CHINESE FIVE-SPICE POWDER

½-INCH/1-CM PIECE FRESH GINGERROOT, GRATED

TO GARNISH

SHREDDED SCALLIONS

SERVES 4

Place the spareribs in a large, shallow, nonmetallic dish. Mix the soy sauce, sugar, oil, garlic, Chinese five-spice powder, and ginger together in a measuring cup. Pour the mixture over the ribs and turn until the ribs are well coated in the marinade.

Cover the dish with plastic wrap and let marinate in the refrigerator for at least 6 hours.

Preheat the barbecue. Drain the ribs, reserving the marinade. Cook over medium hot coals, turning and brushing frequently with the reserved marinade, for 30–40 minutes. Transfer to a large serving dish, garnish with the shredded scallions, and serve immediately.

Alternative Cooking Method

A grill pan or skillet can also be used to cook these ribs. Ensure that you brush the pan with a little oil first and then pre-heat before adding the meat. Cooking times may be increased slightly as this method of cooking does not generate the high heat of a barbecue. You therefore will need to look for visual signs that the food is cooked to your liking.

TANGY PORK RIBS

1¼ TSP SALT

2 TSP PAPRIKA

2 TSP PEPPER

3 LB/1.3 KG PORK RIBS

1 TBSP CHILI OR VEGETABLE OIL

1 ONION, FINELY CHOPPED

6 SCALLIONS, TRIMMED AND
CHOPPED

3 GARLIC CLOVES, CHOPPED

2 TSP FINELY CHOPPED FRESH
GINGERROOT

1 RED CHILI, CHOPPED

1 TBSP CHOPPED FRESH CILANTRO

1 TBSP CHOPPED
FLAT-LEAF PARSLEY

1 TBSP SWEET SHERRY

1½ TBSP BROWN SUGAR

4 TBSP CHINESE
CHILI BEAN SAUCE

1 TBSP TOMATO PASTE

1 TBSP RICE WINE

1 TBSP SHERRY VINEGAR

SCANT ½ CUP ORANGE JUICE

2½ TBSP SOY SAUCE

SALT AND PEPPER

TO SERVE

WEDGES OF ORANGE

SERVES 4

Preheat the oven to 475°F/240°C. Combine the salt, paprika, and pepper in a baking dish and then add the ribs. Turn them in the dish to coat them well all over. Cook in the center of the preheated oven for 1¾–2 hours, then remove the dish from the oven, lift out the ribs, drain off the fat, and set aside.

Heat the oil in a skillet. Add the onion, scallions, garlic, ginger, and chili, and stir-fry over a high heat for 1 minute. Then add the herbs, sherry, sugar, chili bean sauce, tomato paste, rice wine, vinegar, orange juice, and soy sauce. Stir in a large pinch of salt and season well with pepper. Bring to a boil, lower the heat, and simmer for 15–20 minutes, stirring occasionally.

Alternative Cooking Method

To barbecue the ribs, coat them in the sauce, then grill them over hot coals for 7–10 minutes on each side, or until cooked right through, turning them frequently and basting with more sauce as necessary. Serve at once, accompanied by orange wedges.

BARBECUED SPICY PORK RIBS

2 LB/900 G PORK SPARERIBS
⅔ CUP STRAINED TOMATOES
2 TBSP RED WINE VINEGAR
2 TBSP DARK BROWN SUGAR
1 GARLIC CLOVE, CRUSHED
1 TSP DRIED THYME
½ TSP DRIED ROSEMARY
1 TSP CHILI SAUCE

TO GARNISH
FRESH RED CHILIES

TO SERVE
MIXED SALAD LEAVES

SERVES 8

If you buy the spareribs in a single piece, carefully cut them into individual ribs using a very sharp knife. Bring a large pan of water to a boil, add the ribs and cook for 10 minutes, then drain them thoroughly. Place the ribs in a large, shallow, nonmetallic dish.

To make the spicy sauce, mix the strained tomatoes, red wine vinegar, sugar, garlic, thyme, rosemary, and chili sauce together in a bowl until well blended.

Pour the sauce over the pork ribs and toss to coat on all sides. Cover and let marinate in the refrigerator for 1 hour.

Preheat the barbecue. Remove the ribs from the sauce, reserving the sauce for basting. Cook the ribs over hot coals for 5–10 minutes, then move them to a cooler part of the grill. Cook for an additional 15–20 minutes, turning and basting frequently with the remaining sauce. Transfer the ribs to warmed serving plates and garnish with the red chilies, if using. Serve immediately with mixed salad greens.

SPARE RIBS IN
BARBECUE SAUCE

1 LB 2 OZ/500 G PORK FINGER
SPARE RIBS
1 TBSP SUGAR
1 TBSP LIGHT SOY SAUCE
1 TBSP DARK SOY SAUCE
3 TBSP HOISIN SAUCE
1 TBSP RICE WINE OR DRY SHERRY
4-5 TBSP WATER OR
CHINESE STOCK
MILD CHILI SAUCE, TO DIP

TO GARNISH
CILANTRO LEAVES

SERVES 4

Using a sharp knife, trim off any excess fat from the spare ribs
and cut into pieces. Place the ribs in a baking dish.

Mix together the sugar, light and dark soy sauce, hoisin sauce
and wine. Pour over the ribs in the baking dish. Turn to coat the
ribs thoroughly in the mixture and leave to marinate for about
2-3 hours.

Add the water or Chinese stock to the ribs and spread them out
in the dish. Roast in a preheated hot oven for 15 minutes.

Turn the ribs over, lower the oven temperature and cook for
30-35 minutes longer.

To serve, chop each rib into 3-4 small, bite-sized pieces with a
large knife or Chinese cleaver and arrange neatly on a serving dish.

Pour the sauce from the baking dish over the spare ribs and
garnish with a few cilantro leaves. Place some mild chili sauce
into a small dish and serve with the ribs as a dip. Serve immediately.

SPICY RACK OF LAMB
WITH HUMMUS

6 RACKS OF LAMB,
EACH WITH 3 CHOPS
2 TBSP OLIVE OIL

SERVES 6

Preheat the oven to 375°F/190°C. Put the lamb in a roasting pan
and spoon over 2 tbsp of olive oil. Roast for 10–15 minutes, or
until almost cooked through.

MARINADE
1 TBSP OLIVE OIL
2 TBSP HONEY
2 TSP GROUND CORIANDER
2 TSP GROUND CUMIN
1 TSP GROUND ALLSPICE
½ TSP PAPRIKA

Mix together 1 tbsp of olive oil, the honey, coriander, cumin,
allspice, and paprika in a small bowl. Brush the spice mixture all
over the warm lamb, then place in a dish and let cool. Cover
with plastic wrap and let marinate in the refrigerator overnight.

TO GARNISH
FEW SPRIGS OF FRESH MINT

TO SERVE
HUMMUS

Cook the lamb on a medium barbecue, turning frequently, until
heated through and well browned. Alternatively place the lamb
into a preheated oven to 425°F/220°C until heated through and
well browned. Transfer to 6 serving plates, add 2–3 tbsp hummus
to each, garnish with mint sprigs, and serve.

SWEET AND SOUR RIBS

4 SCALLIONS, FINELY CHOPPED

3 TBSP LEMON JUICE

⅔ CUP WHITE WINE VINEGAR

2 TSP ENGLISH MUSTARD

3 TBSP BROWN SUGAR

3 TBSP WORCESTERSHIRE SAUCE

5 TBSP SUNDRIED TOMATO PASTE

2 LB 4 OZ/1 KG PORK SPARERIBS

SALT AND PEPPER

SERVES 4

Put the scallions, lemon juice, vinegar, mustard, sugar, Worcestershire sauce, and sundried tomato paste in a pan, season with salt and pepper, and bring to a boil, stirring well to mix. Reduce the heat and let simmer, stirring occasionally, for 30 minutes. Transfer the pan to the side of the barbecue.

Using a sharp knife, make deep scores all over the racks of ribs, then brush them all over with the sauce.

Grill over a medium barbecue, turning and brushing frequently with the sauce, for 1–1¼ hours, or until cooked through and tender. Serve at once.

SPARE RIBS WITH CHILI

1 LB 2 OZ/500 G PORK SPARE RIBS

1 TSP SUGAR

1 TBSP LIGHT SOY SAUCE

1 TSP RICE WINE OR DRY SHERRY

1 TSP CORNSTARCH

2 CUPS VEGETABLE OIL

1 GARLIC CLOVE, FINELY CHOPPED

1 SCALLION,

CUT INTO SHORT SECTIONS

1 SMALL HOT CHILI PEPPER

(GREEN OR RED), THINLY SLICED

2 TBSP BLACK BEAN SAUCE

SCANT ⅔ CHINESE STOCK OR

WATER

1 SMALL ONION, DICED

1 MEDIUM GREEN BELL PEPPER,

CORED, SEEDED AND DICED

SERVES 4

Trim any excess fat from the ribs. Using a sharp knife or meat cleaver, chop each rib into 3-4 bite-sized piecess and place in a shallow dish.

Mix together the sugar, soy sauce, wine and cornstarch and pour the mixture over the pork ribs. Leave to marinate for 35-45 minutes.

Heat the vegetable oil in a large preheated wok or skillet.

Add the spare ribs to the wok and deep-fry for 2-3 minutes until light brown. Remove with a slotted spoon and drain on absorbent paper towels.

Pour off the oil, leaving about 1 tablespoon in the wok. Add the garlic, scallion, chili pepper and black bean sauce and stir-fry for 30-40 seconds.

Add the spare ribs, blend well, then add the stock or water. Bring to the boil, then reduce the heat, cover and braise for 8-10 minutes, stirring once or twice.

Add the onion and green bell pepper, increase the heat to high, and stir uncovered for about 2 minutes to reduce the sauce a little. Serve hot.

ROASTED SPARE RIBS WITH
HONEY AND SOY

2 LB 4 OZ CHINESE-STYLE
SPARE RIBS

½ LEMON

½ SMALL ORANGE

1 IN PIECE FRESH GINGER,
PEELED

2 GARLIC CLOVES, PEELED

1 SMALL ONION, CHOPPED

2 TBSP SOY SAUCE

2 TBSP RICE WINE

½ TSP THAI SEVEN-SPICE POWDER

2 TBSP HONEY

1 TBSP SESAME OIL

TO GARNISH

LEMON TWISTS

TO SERVE

ORANGE WEDGES

SERVES 4

Place the ribs in a wide roasting pan, cover loosely with foil and cook in an oven preheated to 350°F/175°C for 30 minutes.

Meanwhile, remove any seeds from the lemon and orange and place in a food processor with the ginger, garlic, onion, soy sauce, rice wine, seven-spice powder, honey, and sesame oil. Process until smooth.

Pour off any fat from the spare ribs, then spoon the puréed mixture over the spare ribs. Toss the ribs to coat evenly.

Return the ribs to the oven at 400°F/200°C and roast for about 40 minutes, turning and basting them occasionally, or until golden brown. Serve hot.

LAMB WITH BALSAMIC AND
ROSEMARY MARINADE

6 RACKS OF LAMB,
EACH WITH 3 CHOPS

SERVES 6

MARINADE
3 TBSP CHOPPED FRESH ROSEMARY
1 SMALL ONION, FINELY CHOPPED
3 TBSP OLIVE OIL
1 TBSP BALSAMIC VINEGAR
1 TBSP LEMON JUICE
SALT AND PEPPER

TO GARNISH
FRESH ROSEMARY SPRIGS

Put the lamb in a large, shallow dish and sprinkle with the chopped rosemary and onion. Whisk together the olive oil, balsamic vinegar, and lemon juice and season with salt and pepper.

Pour the balsamic mixture over the lamb, turning well to coat. Cover with plastic wrap and set aside in a cool place to marinate for 1–2 hours.

Drain the lamb, reserving the marinade. Grill the racks, on a medium hot barbecue, brushing frequently with the reserved marinade, for 8–10 minutes on each side. Serve garnished with rosemary sprigs.

Alternative Cooking Method
Place the lamb under a preheated broiler, for 10-12 minutes, depending on the thickness of the meat, or until cooked through. Cooking times may be increased slightly as this method of cooking does not generate the high heat of a barbecue. You therefore will need to look for visual signs that the food is cooked to your liking.

PORK RIBS WITH PLUM SAUCE

2 LB/900 G PORK SPARE RIBS

2 TBSP SUNFLOWER OIL

1 TSP SESAME OIL

2 CLOVES GARLIC, CRUSHED

1 INCH /2.5 CM PIECE FRESH
GINGERROOT, GRATED

⅔ CUP PLUM SAUCE

2 TBSP DRY SHERRY

2 TBSP HOISIN SAUCE

2 TBSP SOY SAUCE

TO GARNISH

4–6 SCALLIONS

SERVES 4

To prepare the garnish, trim the scallions to about 3 inches / 7.5 cm long. Slice both ends into thin strips, leaving the onion intact in the centre.

Put the scallions into a bowl of iced water for at least 30 minutes until the ends start to curl up. Leave them in the water and set aside until required.

If you buy the spare ribs in a single piece, cut them into individual ribs. Bring a large pan of water to the boil and add the ribs. Cook for 5 minutes, then drain thoroughly.

Heat the oils in a pan, add the garlic and ginger and cook gently for 1–2 minutes. Stir in the plum sauce, sherry, hoisin and soy sauce and heat through.

Brush the sauce over the pork ribs. Grill over hot coals for 5–10 minutes, then move to a cooler part of the grill for a further 15–20 minutes, basting with the remaining sauce. Garnish and serve hot.

DEEP-FRIED SPARE RIBS

8-10 FINGER SPARE RIBS

1 TSP FIVE-SPICE POWDER OR

1 TBSP MILD CURRY POWDER

1 TBSP RICE WINE OR DRY SHERRY

1 EGG

2 TBSP FLOUR

VEGETABLE OIL, FOR DEEP-FRYING

1 TSP FINELY SHREDDED
SCALLIONS

1 TSP FINELY SHREDDED FRESH
GREEN OR RED HOT CHILIES,
SEEDED

SALT AND PEPPER

TO SERVE

SPICY SALT AND PEPPER

SERVES 4

Chop the ribs into 3-4 small pieces. Place the ribs in a bowl with salt, pepper, five-spice or curry powder and the wine. Turn to coat the ribs in the spices and leave to marinate for 1-2 hours.

Mix the egg and flour together to make a batter. Dip the ribs in the batter one by one to coat well.

Heat the oil in a preheated wok until smoking. Deep-fry the ribs for 4-5 minutes, then remove with chopsticks or a slotted spoon and drain on paper towels.

Reheat the oil over a high heat and deep-fry the ribs once more for another minute. Remove and drain again on paper towels.

Pour 1 tablespoon of the hot oil over the scallions and chilies and leave for 30-40 seconds. Serve the ribs, garnished with the shredded scallions and chilies.

CLASSIC SPARE RIBS

2 LB/900 G PORK SPARE RIBS
2 TBSP DARK SOY SAUCE
3 TBSP HOISIN SAUCE
1 TBSP CHINESE RICE WINE OR
DRY SHERRY
PINCH OF CHINESE FIVE SPICE
POWDER
2 TSP DARK BROWN SUGAR
¼ TSP CHILI SAUCE
2 GARLIC CLOVES, CRUSHED

TO GARNISH
CILANTRO SPRIGS

SERVES 4

Cut the spare ribs into separate pieces if they are joined together. If desired, you can chop them into 2-inch/5 cm lengths, using a cleaver.

Mix together the soy sauce, hoisin sauce, Chinese rice wine or sherry, Chinese five spice powder, dark brown sugar, chili sauce and garlic in a large bowl.

Place the ribs in a shallow dish and pour the mixture over them, turning to coat them well. Cover and marinate in the refrigerator, turning the ribs from time to time, for at least 1 hour.

Remove the ribs from the marinade and arrange them in a single layer on a wire rack placed over a roasting pan half filled with warm water. Brush with the marinade, reserving the remainder.

Cook in a preheated oven, at 350°F/180°C, for 30 minutes. Remove the roasting pan from the oven and turn the ribs over. Brush with the remaining marinade and return to the oven for a further 30 minutes, or until cooked through. Transfer to a warmed serving dish, garnish with the cilantro sprigs and serve immediately.

BARBECUE RACK OF RIBS

2 RACKS OF PORK RIBS,
ABOUT 1 LB 7 OZ/650 G EACH
VEGETABLE OIL, FOR BRUSHING

SERVES 4-6

FOR THE TENNESSEE RUB
1 TBSP GROUND CUMIN
1 TSP GARLIC SALT
½ TSP GROUND CINNAMON
½ TSP DRY ENGLISH MUSTARD
POWDER
½ TSP GROUND CORIANDER
1 TSP DRIED MIXED HERBS
⅛ TSP CAYENNE PEPPER,
OR TO TASTE

**FOR THE BOURBON BARBECUE
SAUCE**
1 TBSP CORN OR PEANUT OIL
½ ONION, FINELY CHOPPED
2 LARGE GARLIC CLOVES, MINCED
GENEROUS ⅓ CUP PACKED BROWN
SUGAR
1 TBSP DRY ENGLISH MUSTARD
POWDER
1 TSP GROUND CUMIN
2 TBSP TOMATO PASTE
6 TBSP BOURBON
2 TBSP WORCESTERSHIRE SAUCE
2 TBSP APPLE OR WHITE WINE
VINEGAR
FEW DROPS OF HOT PEPPER
SAUCE, TO TASTE

A day ahead, mix all the ingredients for the rub together in a small bowl. Rub the mixture onto both sides of the ribs, then cover and let them marinate in the refrigerator overnight.

To make the barbecue sauce, heat the oil in a pan over a medium-high heat. Add the onion and garlic and cook for 5 minutes, stirring frequently, or until the onion is soft. Stir in the remaining sauce ingredients. Slowly bring to a boil, stirring to dissolve the sugar, then reduce the heat and let simmer, uncovered, for 30 minutes–1 hour, stirring occasionally, until dark brown and very thick. Let cool, then cover and let chill until required.

When ready to barbecue, heat the coals until they are glowing. Brush the barbecue rack with a little oil. Put the ribs onto the rack and cook, turning frequently, for 40 minutes, or until the meat feels tender. If they appear to be drying out, brush with water.

Remove the ribs from the barbecue and cut them into 1 or 2 rib portions. Return the rib portions to the barbecue and brush with the sauce. Cook the ribs, turning frequently and basting generously with the sauce, for an additional 10 minutes, or until they are dark brown and glossy. Serve with a bowl of the hot leftover sauce for dipping – and plenty of paper napkins for sticky fingers!

BITE-SIZE BARBECUED SPARE RIBS

SAUCE

¼ CUP PLUM, HOISIN, SWEET & SOUR, OR DUCK SAUCE

1 TSP BROWN SUGAR

1 TBSP TOMATO KETCHUP

PINCH OF GARLIC POWDER

2 TBSP DARK SOY SAUCE

2 LB 4 OZ/1 KG SPARE RIBS, CHOPPED INTO 2 INCH/5 CM PIECES

TO GARNISH

3 TBSP FRESH, TORN CILANTRO

SERVES 4

Preheat the oven to 375°F/190°C.

To make the sauce, combine the plum or other sauce, brown sugar, ketchup, garlic powder, and soy sauce in a large mixing bowl.

Add the spare ribs to the sauce and stir to coat them thoroughly. Transfer to a metal roasting pan and arrange in a single layer.

Place the roasting pan in the oven and cook the ribs for 20 minutes, or until they are cooked through and sticky. Arrange on a large platter and serve immediately, garnished with cilantro.

SPARERIBS IN A
PINEAPPLE SAUCE

1 LB/450 G SPARERIBS, CUT INTO
BITE-SIZE PIECES

VEGETABLE OR PEANUT
OIL, FOR DEEP-FRYING

FOR THE MARINADE

2 TSP LIGHT SOY SAUCE

½ TSP SALT

PINCH OF WHITE PEPPER

FOR THE SAUCE

3 TBSP WHITE RICE VINEGAR

2 TBSP SUGAR

1 TBSP LIGHT SOY SAUCE

1 TBSP TOMATO KETCHUP

1½ TBSP VEGETABLE.OR
PEANUT OIL

1 GREEN BELL PEPPER,
COARSELY CHOPPED

1 SMALL ONION,
COARSELY CHOPPED

1 SMALL CARROT, FINELY SLICED

½ TSP FINELY CHOPPED GARLIC

½ TSP FINELY CHOPPED GINGER

3½ OZ/100 G PINEAPPLE CHUNKS

SERVES 4

Combine the marinade ingredients in a bowl with the pork and
marinate for at least 20 minutes.

Heat enough oil for deep-frying in a wok, deep-fat fryer or large
heavy-bottom pan until it reaches 350–375°F/180-190°C, or until
a cube of bread browns in 30 seconds. Deep-fry the spareribs for
8 minutes. Drain and set aside.

To prepare the sauce, first mix together the vinegar, sugar, light
soy sauce, and ketchup. Set aside.

In a preheated wok or deep pan, heat 1 tablespoon of the oil and
stir-fry the bell pepper, onion, and carrot for 2 minutes. Remove
and set aside.

In the clean preheated wok or deep pan, heat the remaining oil
and stir-fry the garlic and ginger until fragrant. Add the vinegar
mixture. Bring back to a boil and add the pineapple chunks.
Finally add the spareribs and the bell pepper, onion, and carrot.
Stir until warmed through and serve immediately.

PORK RIBS BRAISED IN SOY SAUCE

1 LB 5 OZ/600 G PORK RIBS,
CUT INTO BITE-SIZE PIECES
1 TBSP DARK SOY SAUCE
1 WHOLE HEAD OF GARLIC
2 TBSP VEGETABLE OR
PEANUT OIL OR SHORTENING
1 CINNAMON STICK
2 STAR ANISE
3 TBSP LIGHT SOY SAUCE
2 OZ/55 G ROCK SUGAR
¾ CUP WATER

SERVES 4

Marinate the pork ribs in the dark soy sauce for at least 20 minutes.

Break the garlic head into cloves, leaving the individual skins intact.

In a preheated wok or deep pan, heat the oil and stir-fry the garlic cloves for 1 minute. Toss in the cinnamon and star anise and stir for an additional minute. Stir in the pork. When the meat is beginning to brown, stir in the light soy sauce, sugar, and water and stir until the sugar is dissolved. Simmer gently, uncovered, for 30 minutes, stirring frequently. Cover and simmer for 60–75 minutes, or until the meat is cooked through and the gravy thick and concentrated.

5 SIDES

I t's hard to imagine roast beef without roast potatoes or steak without French fries, but as well as these traditional accompaniments, this chapter is full of imaginative ideas for vegetables and salads to serve with steaks, chops, roasts, and ribs. What could be tastier than Roasted Garlic Mashed Potatoes (see page 222) with roast lamb, Chargrilled Vegetables with Creamy Pesto (see page 220) with veal chops, or Tropical Rice Salad (see page 226) with grilled pork? From Hush Puppies (see page 230) to Refried Beans (see page 228) and from Coleslaw (see page 242) to Chef's Salad (see page 240), you're sure to find the perfect partner for your meaty main dish.

PERFECT ROAST POTATOES

3 LB/1.3 KG LARGE POTATOES, SUCH AS ROUND WHITE, ROUND RED, OR FINGERLING, PEELED AND CUT INTO EVEN-SIZE CHUNKS

3 TBSP DRIPPING, GOOSE FAT, DUCK FAT, OR OLIVE OIL

SALT

SERVES 6

Preheat the oven to 425°F/220°C.

Cook the potatoes in a large pan of lightly salted boiling water over medium heat, covered, for 5–7 minutes. They will still be firm. Remove from the heat. Meanwhile, add the fat to a roasting pan and place in the hot oven.

Drain the potatoes well and return them to the pan. Cover with the lid and firmly shake the pan so that the surface of the potatoes is slightly roughened to help give them a much crisper texture.

Remove the roasting pan from the oven and carefully tip the potatoes into the hot fat. Baste them to ensure that they are all coated with it.

Roast the potatoes at the top of the oven for 45–50 minutes until they are browned all over and thoroughly crisp. Turn the potatoes and baste again only once during the process or the crunchy edges will be destroyed.

Using a slotted spoon, carefully transfer the potatoes from the roasting pan into a warmed serving dish. Sprinkle with a little salt and serve at once. Any leftovers (although this is most unlikely) are delicious cold.

CHARGRILLED VEGETABLES WITH
CREAMY PESTO

1 RED ONION
1 FENNEL BULB
4 BABY EGGPLANTS
4 BABY ZUCCHINIS
1 ORANGE BELL PEPPER
1 RED BELL PEPPER
2 BEEFSTEAK TOMATOES
2 TBSP OLIVE OIL
SALT AND PEPPER

CREAMY PESTO

4 TBSP FRESH BASIL LEAVES
1 TBSP PINE NUTS
1 GARLIC CLOVE
PINCH OF COARSE SEA SALT
¼ CUP FRESHLY GRATED
PARMESAN CHEESE
¼ CUP EXTRA-VIRGIN OLIVE OIL
⅓ CUP STRAINED PLAIN YOGURT

TO GARNISH

1 FRESH BASIL SPRIG

SERVES 4

Preheat the barbecue. To make the creamy pesto, place the basil, pine nuts, garlic, and sea salt in a mortar and pound to a paste with a pestle. Gradually work in the Parmesan cheese, then gradually stir in the oil. Place the yogurt in a small serving bowl and stir in 3–4 tablespoons of the pesto mixture. Cover with plastic wrap and let chill in the refrigerator until required. Store any leftover pesto mixture in a screw-top jar in the refrigerator.

Prepare the vegetables. Cut the onion and fennel bulb into wedges, trim the eggplants and zucchinis, seed and halve the bell peppers, and cut the tomatoes in half. Brush the vegetables with oil and season to taste with salt and pepper.

Cook the eggplants and bell peppers over hot coals for 3 minutes, then add the zucchinis, onion, and tomatoes and cook, turning occasionally and brushing with more oil if necessary, for an additional 5 minutes. Transfer to a large serving plate and serve with the pesto, garnished with a basil sprig.

Alternative Cooking Method

Preheat a ridged skillet pan over a high heat. Cook the sliced vegetables in turn, griddling until the skins are slightly charred and the flesh is soft (about 2 minutes on each side), brushing with oil if necessary.

ROASTED GARLIC MASHED POTATOES

2 WHOLE BULBS OF GARLIC
1 TBSP OLIVE OIL
2 LB/900 G MEALY POTATOES, PEELED
½ CUP MILK
¼ CUP BUTTER
SALT AND PEPPER

SERVES 4

Preheat the oven to 350°F/180°C.

Separate the garlic cloves, place on a large piece of foil, and drizzle with the oil. Wrap the garlic in the foil and roast in the oven for about 1 hour, or until very tender. Let cool slightly.

Twenty minutes before the end of the cooking time, cut the potatoes into chunks, then cook in salted boiling water for about 15 minutes, or until tender.

Meanwhile, squeeze the cooled garlic cloves out of their skins and push through a strainer into a pan. Add the milk, butter, salt, and pepper and heat gently, until the butter has melted.

Drain the cooked potatoes, then mash in the pan until smooth. Pour in the garlic mixture and heat gently, stirring, until the ingredients are combined. Serve hot.

CORNSTICKS

CORN OIL, FOR OILING

SCANT 1¼ CUPS YELLOW CORNMEAL

¾ CUP ALL-PURPOSE FLOUR, SIFTED

1½–2 TBSP SUPERFINE SUGAR,
TO TASTE

2½ TSP BAKING POWDER

¾ TSP SALT

5 SCALLIONS, FINELY CHOPPED

GENEROUS 1 CUP MILK

1 EGG

TO SERVE

3 TBSP BUTTER, MELTED

MAKES 14

Preheat the oven to 425°F/220°C. Generously brush two 7-stick molds with oil and place them in the oven while it heats.

Do not start mixing the cornmeal batter until the oven has reached the correct temperature. Stir the cornmeal, flour, sugar, baking powder, and salt together in a bowl, then stir in the scallions. Make a well in the center.

Mix the milk, egg, and butter together in a pitcher, then stir into the dry ingredients until just mixed. Do not overmix.

Remove the hot molds from the oven and divide the cornmeal batter between them, filling each mold about three-quarters full. Return the molds to the oven and bake for 20–25 minutes, or until each cornstick is risen and coming away from the side of the mold. A wooden toothpick inserted into the center should come out clean.

Let the cornsticks stand for 1 minute, then use a round-bladed knife to ease them out of the molds. Serve at once with butter for spreading over the cornsticks.

TROPICAL RICE SALAD

½ CUP LONG-GRAIN RICE

SALT AND PEPPER

4 SCALLIONS

8 OZ/225 G CANNED PINEAPPLE
PIECES IN NATURAL JUICE

7 OZ/200 G CANNED CORN, DRAINED

2 RED BELL PEPPERS,
SEEDED AND DICED

3 TBSP GOLDEN RAISINS

DRESSING

1 TBSP PEANUT OIL

1 TBSP HAZELNUT OIL

1 TBSP LIGHT SOY SAUCE

1 GARLIC CLOVE, FINELY CHOPPED

1 TSP CHOPPED FRESH GINGERROOT

SERVES 4

Cook the rice in a large pan of lightly salted boiling water for
15 minutes, or until tender. Drain thoroughly and rinse under
cold running water. Place the rice in a large serving bowl.

Using a sharp knife, finely chop the scallions. Drain the pineapple
pieces, reserving the juice in a measuring cup. Add the pineapple
pieces, corn, red bell peppers, chopped scallions, and golden
raisins to the rice and mix lightly.

Add all the dressing ingredients to the reserved pineapple juice,
whisking well, and season to taste with salt and pepper. Pour the
dressing over the salad and toss until the salad is thoroughly
coated. Serve immediately.

REFRIED BEANS

6–8 TBSP CORN OIL OR SHORTENING

1 ONION, FINELY CHOPPED

1 QUANTITY OF FRIJOLES

TO SERVE

FRIED TORTILLAS

SERVES 6

Heat 2 tablespoons of the corn oil in a large, heavy-bottomed skillet. Add the chopped onion and cook, stirring occasionally, for 5 minutes, or until softened. Add one fourth of the Frijoles.

Mash the Frijoles with a potato masher until well broken up. Add more Frijoles and more oil and mash again. Continue adding Frijoles and oil until all the beans have been incorporated and have formed a solid paste.

Cut the tortillas into fourths. Transfer the refried beans on to a warmed serving dish, shaping the paste into one large roll, and serve immediately, surrounded with the tortillas.

HUSH PUPPIES

1¾ CUPS YELLOW CORNMEAL

½ CUP ALL-PURPOSE FLOUR, SIFTED

1 SMALL ONION, FINELY CHOPPED

1 TBSP SUGAR

2 TSP BAKING POWDER

½ TSP SALT

¾ CUP MILK

1 EGG, BEATEN

CORN OIL, FOR DEEP-FRYING

MAKES ABOUT 36

Stir the cornmeal, flour, onion, sugar, baking powder, and salt together in a bowl and make a well in the center.

Beat the milk and egg together in a pitcher, then pour into the dry ingredients and stir until a thick batter forms.

Heat at least 2 inches/5 cm of oil in a deep skillet or pan over high heat until the temperature reaches 350–375°F/180–190°C, or until a cube of bread browns in 30 seconds.

Drop in as many teaspoonfuls of the batter as will fit without overcrowding the skillet and cook, stirring constantly, until the hush puppies puff up and turn golden.

Remove the hush puppies from the oil with a slotted spoon and drain on paper towels. Reheat the oil, if necessary, and cook the remaining batter. Serve hot.

CANDIED SWEET POTATOES

1 LB 8 OZ/675 G SWEET POTATOES,
SLICED
3 TBSP BUTTER
1 TBSP LIME JUICE
SCANT ⅓ CUP SOFT DARK
BROWN SUGAR
1 TBSP BRANDY
GRATED RIND OF 1 LIME

TO GARNISH
LIME WEDGES

SERVES 6

Cook the sweet potatoes in a large, heavy-bottomed pan of boiling water for 5 minutes, or until softened. To test if the potatoes are soft, prick with a fork. Remove the sweet potatoes with a perforated spoon and drain thoroughly.

Melt the butter in a large skillet. Add the lime juice and sugar and heat gently, stirring, to dissolve the sugar.

Stir the sweet potatoes and the brandy into the sugar and lime juice mixture. Cook over low heat for 10 minutes, or until the potato slices are cooked through.

Sprinkle the lime rind over the top of the sweet potatoes and mix well.

Transfer the candied sweet potatoes to a large, warmed serving plate. Garnish with lime wedges and serve immediately.

BLACK BEAN NACHOS

1¼ CUPS DRIED BLACK BEANS, OR
1⅔ CUPS CANNED BLACK BEANS,
DRAINED AND RINSED
1½–2 CUPS GRATED CHEESE,
SUCH AS CHEDDAR
ABOUT ¼ TSP CUMIN SEEDS OR
GROUND CUMIN
ABOUT 4 TBSP SOUR CREAM
THINLY SLICED PICKLED
JALAPEÑOS (OPTIONAL)
1 TBSP CHOPPED FRESH CILANTRO
HANDFUL OF SHREDDED LETTUCE

TO SERVE
TORTILLA CHIPS

SERVES 4

If using dried black beans, place them in a bowl and add water to cover. Set aside to soak overnight, then drain. Put in a pan, cover with water, and bring to a boil. Boil for 10 minutes, then reduce the heat, and simmer for about 1½ hours until tender. Drain well.

Spread the cooked or canned beans in the base of a shallow casserole, then sprinkle the cheese over the top. Sprinkle with cumin to taste.

Bake in a preheated oven, 375°F/190°C, for 10–15 minutes or until the beans are cooked through and the cheese is bubbling and melted.

Remove the beans and cheese from the oven and spoon the sour cream on top. Add the jalapeños, if using, and sprinkle with fresh cilantro and lettuce.

Arrange the tortilla chips around the beans, sticking them into the mixture. Serve the nachos at once.

GARLIC POTATO
WEDGES

3 LARGE BAKING POTATOES,
SCRUBBED
4 TBSP OLIVE OIL
2 TBSP BUTTER
2 GARLIC CLOVES, CHOPPED
1 TBSP CHOPPED FRESH ROSEMARY
1 TBSP CHOPPED FRESH PARSLEY
1 TBSP CHOPPED FRESH THYME
SALT AND PEPPER

SERVES 4

Bring a large pan of water to a boil. Add the potatoes and parboil them for 10 minutes. Drain the potatoes and refresh under cold water, then drain them again thoroughly.

Transfer the potatoes to a cutting board. When the potatoes are cold enough to handle, cut them into thick wedges, but do not peel.

Heat the oil and butter in a small pan together with the garlic. Cook gently until the garlic begins to brown, then remove the pan from the heat.

Stir the herbs and salt and pepper to taste into the mixture in the pan.

Brush the herb mixture all over the potato wedges.

Grill the potatoes over hot coals for 10-15 minutes, brushing liberally with any of the remaining herb and butter mixture, or until the potato wedges are just tender.

Transfer the garlic potato wedges to a warm serving plate and serve as an appetizer or as a side dish.

Alternative Cooking Method
Preheat the oven to 425°F/220°C. Place wedges into a roasting tin and cook for 35-45 minutes until golden and crispy.

CORN-ON-THE-COB

4 CORN COBS, WITH HUSKS
3½ OZ/100 G BUTTER
1 TBSP CHOPPED FRESH PARSLEY
1 TSP CHOPPED FRESH CHIVES
1 TSP CHOPPED FRESH THYME
GRATED RIND OF 1 LEMON
SALT AND PEPPER

SERVES 4

Preheat the barbecue. To prepare the corn cobs, peel back the husks and remove the silken hairs. Fold the husks back around the kernels and secure them in place with string if necessary.

Blanch the corn cobs in a large pan of boiling water for 5 minutes. Remove with a perforated spoon and drain thoroughly. Cook the corn cobs over medium hot coals for 20–30 minutes, turning frequently.

Meanwhile, soften the butter and beat in the parsley, chives, thyme, lemon rind, and salt and pepper to taste. Transfer the corn cobs to serving plates, remove the string, and pull back the husks. Serve each with a generous portion of herb butter.

Alternative Cooking Method

Cook the cobs in boiling water or steam for 10-12 minutes. When cooked the kernels should feel tender when pierced.

CHEF'S SALAD

1 ICEBERG LETTUCE, SHREDDED

6 OZ/175 G COOKED HAM,
CUT INTO THIN STRIPS

6 OZ/175 G COOKED TONGUE,
CUT INTO THIN STRIPS

12 OZ/350 G COOKED CHICKEN,
CUT INTO THIN STRIPS

6 OZ/175 G SWISS CHEESE

4 TOMATOES, QUARTERED

3 HARD-COOKED EGGS, SHELLED
AND QUARTERED

1¼ CUPS THOUSAND ISLAND
DRESSING

SERVES 6

Arrange the lettuce on a large serving platter. Arrange the cold meat decoratively on top.

Cut the Swiss cheese into thin sticks, sprinkle over the salad, and arrange the tomato and egg quarters round the edge of the platter.

Serve the salad immediately, and serve the dressing separately.

COLESLAW

SERVES 4-6

8 OZ/225 G WHITE CABBAGE, CORED AND GRATED

8 OZ/225 G CARROTS, PEELED AND GRATED

4 TBSP SUGAR

3 TBSP CIDER VINEGAR

½ CUP HEAVY CREAM, LIGHTLY WHIPPED

2 PICKLED GREEN OR RED BELL PEPPERS, DRAINED AND THINLY SLICED (OPTIONAL)

4 TBSP FINELY CHOPPED FRESH PARSLEY

SALT AND PEPPER

Combine the cabbage, carrots, sugar, vinegar, a large pinch of salt, and pepper to taste in a large bowl, tossing the ingredients together. Cover and let chill for 1 hour.

Stir all the ingredients together well. Lightly stir in the whipped cream and the pickled bell peppers, if using. Taste and add extra sugar, vinegar, or salt, if desired. Sprinkle over the parsley and serve at once. Alternatively, cover and let chill until required.

POTATO SKINS WITH GUACAMOLE

4 LARGE BAKING POTATOES

2 TSP OLIVE OIL

COARSE SEA SALT AND PEPPER

GUACAMOLE DIP

6 OZ/175 G RIPE AVOCADO

1 TBSP LEMON JUICE

2 RIPE, FIRM TOMATOES, CHOPPED FINELY

1 TSP GRATED LEMON RIND

3½ OZ/100 G LOWFAT SOFT CHEESE WITH HERBS AND GARLIC

4 SCALLIONS, CHOPPED FINELY

A FEW DROPS OF TABASCO SAUCE

SALT AND PEPPER

TO GARNISH

CHOPPED FRESH CHIVES

SERVES 4

Bake the potatoes in a preheated oven at 400°F/200°C for 1¼ hours. Remove from the oven and allow to cool for 30 minutes. Reset the oven to 425°F/220°C.

Halve the potatoes lengthwise and scoop out 2 tablespoons of the flesh. Slice in half again. Place on a cookie sheet and brush the flesh side lightly with oil. Sprinkle with salt and pepper. Bake for a further 25 minutes until golden and crisp.

To make the guacamole dip, mash the avocado with the lemon juice. Add the remaining ingredients and mix.

Drain the potato skins on paper towels and transfer to a warmed serving platter. Garnish with chives. Pile the avocado mixture into a serving bowl.

SPICY RICE

3 TBSP OLIVE OIL

6 SCALLIONS, CHOPPED

1 CELERY STALK, FINELY CHOPPED

3 GARLIC CLOVES, FINELY CHOPPED

2 GREEN BELL PEPPERS, SEEDED AND CHOPPED

CORN KERNELS, CUT FROM 1 EAR FRESH CORN

2 FRESH MILD GREEN CHILIES, SEEDED AND FINELY CHOPPED

GENEROUS 1¼ CUPS LONG-GRAIN RICE

2 TSP GROUND CUMIN

2½ CUPS CHICKEN OR VEGETABLE STOCK

2 TBSP CHOPPED FRESH CILANTRO

SALT AND PEPPER

TO GARNISH

FRESH CILANTRO SPRIGS

SERVES 4

Heat the oil in a large, heavy-bottom pan over medium heat. Add the scallions, celery, and garlic and cook for 5 minutes, or until softened. Add the bell peppers, corn, and chilies and cook for 5 minutes.

Add the rice and cumin and cook, stirring to coat the grains in the oil, for 2 minutes.

Stir in the stock and half the chopped cilantro and bring to a boil. Reduce the heat, cover, and let simmer for 15 minutes, or until nearly all the liquid has been absorbed and the rice is just tender.

Remove from the heat and fluff up with a fork. Stir in the remaining chopped cilantro and season to taste with salt and pepper. Let stand, covered, for 5 minutes before serving. Serve garnished with cilantro sprigs.

HOME-MADE OVEN FRENCH FRIES

1 LB/450 G POTATOES, PEELED

2 TBSP SUNFLOWER OIL

SALT AND PEPPER

SERVES 4

Preheat the oven to 400°F/200°C.

Cut the potatoes into thick, even-sized sticks. Rinse them under cold running water and then dry well on a clean dish towel. Put in a bowl, add the oil, and toss together until coated.

Spread the fries on a cookie sheet and cook in the oven for 40–45 minutes, turning once, until golden. Add salt and pepper to taste, and serve hot.

POTATO, ARUGULA AND MOZZARELLA SALAD

1 LB 7 OZ/650 G SMALL
NEW POTATOES

4½ OZ/125 G ARUGULA LEAVES

5½ OZ/150 G FIRM MOZZARELLA

1 LARGE PEAR

1 TBSP LEMON JUICE

SALT AND PEPPER

DRESSING

3 TBSP EXTRA-VIRGIN OLIVE OIL

1½ TBSP WHITE WINE VINEGAR

1 TSP SUGAR

PINCH OF MUSTARD POWDER

SERVES 4

Bring a pan of salted water to a boil. Add the potatoes, reduce the heat and cook for about 15 minutes, or until tender. Remove from the heat, drain, and set aside to cool.

When the potatoes are cool, halve them, and place them in a large salad bowl. Wash and drain the arugula leaves, cut the mozzarella into cubes, and wash, trim, and slice the pear. Add them to the bowl along with the lemon juice. Season with salt and pepper.

To make the dressing, mix together the oil, vinegar, sugar, and mustard powder. Pour the dressing over the salad and toss all the ingredients together until they are well coated. Serve at once.

RÖSTI

1 LB/450 G MEALY POTATOES
1 MEDIUM ONION, GRATED
SALT AND PEPPER
OIL FOR SHALLOW FRYING

SERVES 4

Wash the potatoes, but do not peel them. Place in a large pan, cover with water, and bring to a boil, covered, over high heat. Reduce the heat and simmer for about 10 minutes, until the potatoes are just beginning to soften. Be careful not to overcook.

Drain the potatoes. Let cool, then peel, and grate coarsely. Mix the grated onion with the potatoes. Season the mixture with salt and pepper.

Heat the oil in a heavy skillet and spoon in the potato mixture. The rösti can be as thick or as thin as you like, and can be made into 1 large cake or several individual ones.

Cook over high heat for about 5 minutes, until the bottom is golden, then turn, and cook until the second side is brown and crispy. Remove from the heat, drain, and serve.

INDEX

A

apples
  apple sauce 134
  Neapolitan veal cutlets with
    mascarpone 68
  pork steaks with mustard and
    apple 36
  salsa 179
apricots: stuffed pork fillet 128
avocados
  guacamole 244
  Mexican steak with avocado
    salsa 22

B

bacon
  pot roasted leg of lamb 144
  stuffed roast pork with garlic 158
beans
  black bean nachos 234
  pork chops and spicy beans 114
  refried beans 228
  roast lamb with beans 168
beef 7, 8
  beef with bell pepper and
    tomatoes 60
  beef with exotic mushrooms 28
  boozy beef steaks 52
  festive beef Wellington 160
  ginger beef with chili 62
  grilled steak with hot chili salsa 18
  marinated sirloin 38
  Mexican steak with avocado
    salsa 22
  mustard steaks with tomato
    relish 42
  New Orleans steak sandwich 34
  pepper steak 30
  roast beef 170
  rump steak with dark barbecue
    sauce 48
  sauerbraten 152
  steak with blue cheese topping 54
  steak with country gravy 50
  steak packages 56
  steaks in orange sauce 26
  steaks with red onion 64
  Tabasco steaks with watercress
    butter 14
  tequila-marinated beef steaks 46
bell peppers
  beef with bell pepper and
    tomatoes 60
  chargrilled vegetables with creamy
    pesto 220
  coleslaw 242

ginger beef with chili 62
roast pork in soy sauce 146
spare ribs with chili 196
spareribs in a pineapple sauce 212
spicy rice 246
tropical rice salad 226

C

capers
  Italian marinated pork chops 86
  veal chops with salsa verde 118
  vitello tonnato 136
celery
  lamb shanks braised with garlic 142
  pot roasted leg of lamb 144
  pot-roast pork 172
  spicy rice 246
cheese
  black bean nachos 234
  chef's salad 240
  guacamole 244
  herbed pork chops 72
  Neapolitan veal cutlets with
    mascarpone 68
  New Orleans steak sandwich 34
  pork stuffed with prosciutto 132
  potato, arugula and mozzarella
    salad 250
  steak with blue cheese topping 54
chilies
  barbecued spicy pork ribs 188
  deep-fried spare ribs 204
  ginger beef with chili 62
  grilled steak with hot chili salsa 18
  hot and spicy ribs 176
  lamb shanks braised with garlic 142
  Mexican steak with avocado
    salsa 22
  pork chops and spicy beans 114
  spare ribs with chili 196
  spicy rice 246
  tangy pork ribs 186
cider
  maple roast lamb with cider 162
  roast lamb with beans 168
coconut
  Caribbean pork 94
  pork steaks with lemon-grass 24
coleslaw 242
cornmeal
  cornsticks 224
  hush puppies 230
cream
  black bean nachos 234
  coleslaw 242
  pepper steak 30

pork chops and spicy beans 114
pot-roast pork 172
steak with country gravy 50
Cumberland sauce 154

E

eggplants
  butterfly chops with red currant
    glaze 78
  chargrilled vegetables with creamy
    pesto 220
  lamb with eggplant 92
  pork chops and spicy beans 114

F

fennel
  chargrilled vegetables with creamy
    pesto 220
  pork with fennel and juniper 106
  slow-roasted pork 126

G

garlic
  garlic potato wedges 236
  lamb shanks braised with garlic 142
  roast lamb with garlic and
    rosemary 138
  roasted garlic mashed potatoes 222
  stuffed roast pork with garlic 158
gin
  gin and juniper pork 80
  marinated lamb chops 96
gingeroot
  Chinese ribs 184
  ginger beef with chili 62
  honey-glazed pork chops 108
  hot and spicy ribs 176
  marinated roast lamb 166
  minted lamb chops 84
  pork chops and spicy beans 114
  pork ribs with plum sauce 202
  roast loin of pork 122
  roast pork in soy sauce 146
  roasted red pork 150
  roasted spare ribs with honey and
    soy 198
  spareribs in a pineapple sauce 212
  tangy pork ribs 186

H

ham
  baked ham with sauce 140
  chef's salad 240
  glazed ham steaks 20
  ham steak in Madeira sauce 44
  pork stuffed with prosciutto 132

roast ham 154
oney
cha siu 130
honey-glazed pork chops 108
roasted spare ribs with honey and
soy 198
spicy rack of lamb with
hummus 192
stuffed roast pork with garlic 158

J

uniper berries
gin and juniper pork 80
marinade 10
pork with fennel and juniper 106
pot-roast pork 172

L

amb 7, 8-9
barbecued lamb ribs 182
butterfly chops with red currant
glaze 78
crusted rack of lamb 178
Italian lamb chops 100
lamb with balsamic and rosemary
marinade 200
lamb with bay and lemon 74
lamb chops with rosemary 110
lamb with eggplant 92
lamb shanks braised with garlic 142
lamb shanks with roasted
onions 164
lamb with zucchini and
tomatoes 70
maple roast lamb with cider 162
marinated lamb chops 96
marinated roast lamb 166
minted lamb chops 84
Persian lamb chops 82
pot roasted leg of lamb 144
rack of lamb 180
roast lamb with beans 168
roast lamb with garlic and
rosemary 138
roast lamb with rosemary and
Marsala 156
roast tomato and lamb packets 88
slow-cooked lamb with orzo 148
spicy lamb steaks 16
spicy rack of lamb with
hummus 192
stuffed shoulder of lamb 124
lemon-grass: pork steaks with
lemon-grass 24
lemons
corn-on-the-cob 238
crusted rack of lamb 178
gremolata 104
lamb with bay and lemon 74

pork in lemon sauce 112
roasted spare ribs with honey and
soy 198
stuffed shoulder of lamb 124
limes
candied sweet potatoes 232
gremolata 104
hot and spicy ribs 176
lamb shanks braised with garlic 142
tequila-marinated beef steaks 46

M

Madeira
ham steak in Madeira sauce 44
marinade 10
veal chops with wild mushroom
sauce 116
maple syrup: maple roast lamb with
cider 162
marinades 10
mint
crusted rack of lamb 178
mint sauce 180
minted lamb chops 84
Persian lamb chops 82
salsa 220
mushrooms
beef with exotic mushrooms 28
festive beef Wellington 160
Neapolitan veal cutlets with
mascarpone 68
stuffed roast pork with garlic 158
veal chops with wild mushroom
sauce 116
mustard
baked ham with sauce 140
barbecued lamb ribs 182
bourbon barbecue sauce 208
glazed ham steaks 20
ham steak in Madeira sauce 44
marinated lamb chops 96
marinated sirloin 38
mustard steaks with tomato
relish 42
New Orleans steak sandwich 34
pork steaks with mustard and
apple 36
roast beef 170
roast ham 154
rump steak with dark barbecue
sauce 48
steak with blue cheese topping 54
steak packages 56
steaks with red onion 64
sweet and sour ribs 194

N

nutritional content 7-8

nuts
Caribbean pork 94
herbed pork chops 72

O

olives
lamb with eggplant 92
Neapolitan pork steaks 32
pork stuffed with prosciutto 132
pork in white wine and olive
sauce 58
vitello tonnato 136
oranges
baked ham with sauce 140
Cumberland sauce 154
gin and juniper pork 80
honey-glazed pork chops 108
pork with fennel and juniper 106
pork with orange sauce 104
roasted spare ribs with honey and
soy 198
steaks in orange sauce 26
steaks with red onion 64
tangy pork ribs 186
tequila-marinated beef steaks 46

P

peaches: Virginian pork chops 98
pears
potato, arugula and mozzarella
salad 250
roast loin of pork 122
peppercorns
pepper steak 30
Virginian pork chops 98
pesto 220
pineapples
ginger beef with chili 62
glazed ham steaks 20
spareribs in a pineapple sauce 212
tropical rice salad 226
pork 7, 9
barbecue rack of ribs 208
barbecued spicy pork ribs 188
bite-size barbecued spare ribs 210
Caribbean pork 94
cha siu 130
Chinese ribs 184
classic spare ribs 206
deep-fried spare ribs 204
gin and juniper pork 80
herbed pork chops 72
honey-glazed pork chops 108
hot and spicy ribs 176
Italian marinated pork chops 86
Neapolitan pork steaks 32
pork chops with sage 102
pork chops and spicy beans 114
pork with fennel and juniper 106

pork in lemon sauce 112
pork with orange sauce 104
pork ribs braised in soy sauce 214
pork ribs with plum sauce 202
pork steaks with lemon-grass 24
pork steaks with mustard and
  apple 36
pork stuffed with prosciutto 132
pork in white wine and olive
  sauce 58
pot-roast pork 172
roast loin of pork 122
roast pork with crackling 134
roast pork in soy sauce 146
roasted red pork 150
roasted spare ribs with honey and
  soy 198
slow-roasted pork 126
spare ribs in barbecue sauce 190
spare ribs with chili 196
spareribs in a pineapple sauce 212
sticky pork chops 90
stuffed pork fillet 128
stuffed roast pork with garlic 158
stuffed shoulder of lamb 124
sweet and sour ribs 194
tangy pork ribs 186
Virginian pork chops 98
potatoes
  garlic potato wedges 236
  oven French fries 248
  potato, arugula and mozzarella
    salad 250
  potato skins with guacamole 244
  roast potatoes 218
  roasted garlic mashed potatoes 222
  rösti 252
prunes: stuffed pork fillet 128

R

red currant jelly
  baked ham with sauce 140
  butterfly chops with red currant
    glaze 78
  Cumberland sauce 154
  rack of lamb 180
  roast lamb with garlic and
    rosemary 138
rice
  spicy rice 246
  tropical rice salad 226
rosemary
  garlic potato wedges 236
  lamb with balsamic and rosemary
    marinade 200
  lamb chops with rosemary 110
  lamb shanks with roasted
    onions 164
  pot roasted leg of lamb 144

rack of lamb 180
roast lamb with garlic and
  rosemary 138
roast lamb with rosemary and
  Marsala 156
stuffed shoulder of lamb 124

S

sage
  festive beef Wellington 160
  Italian marinated pork chops 86
  pork chops with sage 102
  roast lamb with rosemary and
    Marsala 156
  roast loin of pork 122
  stuffed roast pork with garlic 158
soy sauce
  bite-size barbecued spare ribs 210
  cha siu 180
  Chinese ribs 184
  classic spare ribs 206
  ginger beef with chili 62
  hot and spicy ribs 176
  pork ribs braised in soy sauce 214
  pork ribs with plum sauce 202
  roast pork in soy sauce 146
  roasted red pork 150
  roasted spare ribs with honey and
    soy 198
  spare ribs in barbecue sauce 190
  spare ribs with chili 196
  spareribs in a pineapple sauce 212
  sticky pork chops 90
  tangy pork ribs 186
sweet potatoes
  candied sweet potatoes 232
  sweet potato mash 179
sweetcorn
  corn-on-the-cob 238
  spicy rice 246
  tropical rice salad 226

T

tabbouleh 83
tomatoes
  beef with bell pepper and
    tomatoes 60
  chargrilled vegetables with creamy
    pesto 220
  chef's salad 240
  guacamole 244
  Italian lamb chops 100
  lamb with eggplant 92
  lamb with zucchini and
    tomatoes 70
  mustard steaks with tomato
    relish 42
  Neapolitan pork steaks 32
  New Orleans steak sandwich 34

pork chops with sage 102
pot roasted leg of lamb 144
roast tomato and lamb packets 88
rump steak with dark barbecue
  sauce 48
salsa 18, 179
slow-cooked lamb with orzo 148
spicy lamb steaks 16
sweet and sour ribs 194
tuna: vitello tonnato 136

V

veal 7, 9
  Neapolitan veal cutlets with
    mascarpone 68
  stuffed shoulder of lamb 124
  veal chops with salsa verde 118
  veal chops with wild mushroom
    sauce 116
  veal with pickled vegetables 76
  vitello tonnato 136
vegetables
  chargrilled vegetables with creamy
    pesto 220
  coleslaw 242
  sauerbraten 152
  veal with pickled vegetables 76
  see also individual vegetables
venison 7
  chargrilled venison steaks 40

W

watercress: Tabasco steaks with
  watercress butter 14

Y

yogurt
  marinated roast lamb 166
  minted lamb chops 84
  Persian lamb chops 82
  pesto 220
Yorkshire pudding 170

Z

zucchini
  chargrilled vegetables with creamy
    pesto 220
  lamb with zucchini and
    tomatoes 70